Phil Robinson

Fishes of Fancy : their place in myth, fable, Fairy-tale and Folk-lore :

with notices of the Fishes of legendary art, Astronomy and heraldry

Phil Robinson

Fishes of Fancy : their place in myth, fable, Fairy-tale and Folk-lore :
with notices of the Fishes of legendary art, Astronomy and heraldry

ISBN/EAN: 9783744789943

Printed in Europe, USA, Canada, Australia, Japan

Cover: Foto ©Suzi / pixelio.de

More available books at **www.hansebooks.com**

International Fisheries Exhibition

LONDON, 1883

FISHES OF FANCY

THEIR PLACE IN MYTH, FABLE, FAIRY-TALE AND FOLK-LORE

WITH

NOTICES OF THE FISHES OF LEGENDARY ART, ASTRONOMY AND HERALDRY

BY

PHIL ROBINSON

AUTHOR OF "IN MY INDIAN GARDEN," "UNDER THE PUNKAH," "NOAH'S
ARK—AN ESSAY IN UNNATURAL HISTORY," "SINNERS AND
SAINTS," "THE POET'S BIRDS," ETC., ETC.

LONDON

WILLIAM CLOWES AND SONS, LIMITED

INTERNATIONAL FISHERIES EXHIBITION

AND 13 CHARING CROSS, S.W.

1883

PREFATORY NOTE.

THE range of this Handbook is so extensive, that it is obviously impossible to accomplish more than a superficial review of its subjects in the compass of ninety pages. For it traverses Primitive Zoolatry (glancing at Totemism and Sacred Fish-myths), Zoological Mythology, Legendary Art, the Folk-tale of all nations, Fables, the Sciences of Heraldry and Astronomy—and Modern Folklore. Moreover, following the liberal "fish-idea" of the Exhibition, it has been necessary to wander from the cetaceans on the one hand through fishes proper to the crustacea and molluscs on the other. So that not only in Unnatural, but in Natural History also, the range of this Handbook is of necessity very wide. I have contented myself, therefore, with bringing a few leading thoughts into prominence—the antiquity of the Religious Fish-myth, its dignity, its importance in Totemism, the benign aspect of Fish in the Folk-tale, the persistence of ancient fancies in modern superstitions. Such subjects are not, I take it, to be treated with a uniform gravity ; at the same time their intrinsic importance should never be lost sight of. It is in this humour that I have written, and fully conscious that the magnitude of the matters of which I have to treat—Animism in its largest and latest aspects—

makes it impossible here, in so limited a space, to say all I should, would, or could. I would, therefore, anticipate my critics, by saying, that the value of this Handbook is in what it omits rather than in what it contains. It has in it the suggestions for a very desirable volume.

PHIL ROBINSON.

CONTENTS.

THE FISHES OF FANCY.

" Where hast thou floated, in what seas pursued
Thy pastime ? "—*Cowper.*

FISHES OF FANCY.

CHAPTER I.

PRIMITIVE FISH-BELIEFS.

The loss of Solomon's work on Fish a possible misfortune—Reticence
in Holy Writ as to Fish—Even St. Peter does not identify his
Fishes—The First Fishers—Dignities of Fishes and their Antiquity
—How they chose Leviathan king, and how the Monarchy is now
a Republic—Individual Fishes of Honour and of Disrepute—That
the Sea is a duplicate of the Earth, an error ; but resemblances
not to be despised—That Birds were once Fish—Romance of Fact
—Are not the Popular Ideas about Fishes prejudiced by error ?—
What Fishes might think of us.

THAT the world sustained a great loss in the destruction
of Solomon's work on Fishes may be accepted as beyond
dispute, for let the scientific attainments of the sumptuous
builder have been what they might, there can be no doubt
of it, Solomon, who was of an artistic kind, would have
preserved to posterity a vast quantity of old-world nonsense,
possibly even of antediluvian facts, which is now hopelessly
lost to us ; and except Solomon, no other personage of
Holy Writ has expatiated on the subject of fishes. We
have no scriptural recognition of any great fisher "before
the Lord." Indeed, the untranslated Bible is singularly
reticent on the subject, for it does not specify a single fish.
Tobit's fish and Jonah's fish, the fishes of the Psalms and
of the New Testament, are spoken of only generically, and
even when the Lawgiver is enumerating the things which

the Hebrews might and might not eat, he is careful to distinguish by their names the creatures in fur and feathers, but the fish are merely divided into "those with scales and fins," and "those without." Still more remarkable is it that Peter and his comrades, themselves professional fishermen, should have omitted to identify the actual species with which the Saviour worked His miracles. In fish history, therefore, there is a very considerable gap, and it is not until we go to Pagan Mythology that we find the things of the water identified into species.

Of fishing itself we have records from the earliest times, for the Vedas, and of course the Bible, speak of the net and line, spear and hook. But the first of fishers of whom any record remains is undoubtedly that primæval god of the ichthyophagous Polynesians who existed in the very beginning, and when first heard of was out a-fishing on the face of the waters. And he fished up dry land with a hook and line—

> " His hook he baited with a dragon's tail,
> And sat upon a rock, and bobb'd for whale."

Coeval with this deity were those mighty anglers Thor and Odin, who fished (sometimes for the sea-serpent itself) in the Scandinavian seas. Judging, however, from the fact that in the East the caste is still one of very low degree, and that in the most primitive communities, fish-catching is still the work of women—and so distinguished from other kinds of sport, which are always the first and proudest privilege of savage manhood—it is not likely that the private angler was an individual of any importance. Coming down, however, to the classical period, we find the pastime established in popularity and fashion. Kings and their courts amused themselves with the spear and net. Agrippa was so fond of fishing that he called himself Neptune. The Emperors of Rome practised it with every circumstance of characteristic luxury : their nets were of purple silk, and the ropes of gilt twine. It is true that "from time immemorial" the Emperors of China had gone a-fishing, and not less a fact that Gulliver found folk fishing both in Brobdingnag and in Liliput. "But the people of the former country did not care for sea-fish ; they were all the ordinary size. Sometimes, though, they caught a whale, and I have known them so large that a man could hardly carry one upon his shoulders ; and sometimes, for curiosity, they are brought in hampers to Lorbrulgrud." What they caught in Liliput he does not tell us.

Izaak Walton—"that quaint old coxcomb"—I know, amuses himself by surmising that Seth, the son of Adam, taught his son to cast a fly, and that he engraved the mystery of the craft upon those pillars of which Masons and Mormons know so much. But the world in general will hardly be content to believe that the patriarch really occupied so much valuable surface with the details of fishing, and will prefer to accept the imperial masters of Rome as the first of gentlemen anglers, and the fascinating Cleopatra as the first of the fair sex who made angling a feminine fashion.

Apart from their historical records, the fishes have held a really important place in the world's attention from the beginning of time. This, at any rate, is beyond doubt, that the oldest folk-lore extant, the Buddhist, abounds in morals and significances drawn from the finny race, and that one of the oldest of worships, the Phallic, finds under the symbol of these creatures a conspicuous expression. Wherever we go in the East, we find them in Art and Literature perpetually recurrent. It was in the First Age of the World (so spake the Buddha when reproving the luxurious Monk of Jetavana) that the fishes chose Leviathan for their king. Aqueous society, therefore, was an established monarchy at the earliest possible date. What manner of thing "Leviathan" was in those unevoluted days—the period called (until the days of Lyell) the Epoch of Diluvium and Catastrophe, the age of unlimited mud—it would be almost profane for us, in these puny days of whales, without spirit enough in us to firk up even a sea-serpent, to attempt to imagine ; and for myself I am content to believe with the Talmudists that it was an indefinable sea-monster, of which the female lay coiled round the earth, till God, fearing her progeny might destroy the new globe, killed it, and that then He salted her flesh and put it away for the banquet which the pious shall enjoy at the Great End. In that day the angel Gabriel will kill the male also, and will make a tent out of his skin for the elect that are bidden to the banquet. It is a hazy old tradition, I confess, but it is the oldest we have, and, as regards Leviathan, quite as satisfactory as any other on the subject.

But the monarchy must have collapsed, for fishes are nowadays distinctly republican, and each arrives at its own particular measure of dignity upon grounds apart from any relation to a central authority. An Arabic legend * tells us of the Lake Biserta, which received twelve different kinds of fish, one for each month of the year, without any intermixture, for when their month elapsed all the fish of the species then in possession used to vacate the lake, and were replaced by another. But this admirable system of methodical tenancy—reminding one of the system in vogue in rest-houses in the East, where a party

* Now for the first time in print, as are most of the others in this Handbook from Arabic sources.

of travellers can only remain twenty-four hours, and on the arrival of the next party has to move on, bag and baggage—does not obtain anywhere else, for fish are now thoroughly American in their confusion of classes and the assertion of their disregard for each other's liberty.

In the general struggle some of them have attained to honours by their force of character. For instance, the salmon—so lordly in its nature as to worthily justify the name of that proud King of Elis who defied Olympus. But he was hurled to the shades by a judiciously-directed thunderbolt, and thus abundantly expiated his arrogant obliquities. So too the shark, that awful Attila of the sea ; and the pike also, the dispeopler of the lake, that by its ferocity of countenance and manners usurps the autocracy of the reedy waters, and compels the vigilance not only of the otter that comes to poach, but of the beasts of man that come to drink, and even of man himself ; for it has been known to rout the "goose-footed prowler," to bite off a swan's head, to seize the nose of a drinking cow, and, crowning audacity, to bite man. Did not Theodoric the Goth die of fright at seeing a pike's head on his table ? He mistook it for the head of a person whom he had that day unjustly put to death.

Other fish, again, have compassed dignity by the passive virtues of their flesh. Did not Domitian order a special session of the Senate to discuss the cooking of a turbot, and "nihil ad rhombum " — all Lombard Street to a China orange—pass into a proverb ? What man in Rome would not have been a lamprey to be petted by the beautiful wife of Drusus ? and what a pitch of dignity they attained to in the households of epicures, those mullet and muræna and carp !

But by far the greater number have achieved distinction

by legendary exploits, or by accidents of honour. Thus
the dolphin and the tortoise, or the haddock and the John
Dory. It was a crab that retrieved the crucifix of St.
Xavier from the sea—

> " Nor let Xavier's great wonders pass concealed,
>   How storms were by the almighty wafer quelled ;
>   How zealous crab the sacred image bore,
>   And swam a catholic to the distant shore ;"

and to a codfish that Scandinavia owed its recovered
crown. Was it not a fish that guided the Vedic ark to its
resting-place, the hill-peak Naubandha ? and from a fish-
pond (according to Arabic legend) that Moses was rescued
by Pharaoh's daughter ? When the demons had usurped
Solomon's throne, and the monarch was an outcast in his
dominions and jeered at as a sort of Perkin Warbeck, a
preposterous claimant, a fish found the omnipotent signet-
ring, and so enabled the king to reascend his throne. Did
they not give their names to a score of cities ? Is not fish
one of the special foods promised to the faithful in the
paradise of the Moslem, with, hard by, that tree from Sinai
that yields sauces "for them who eat"—a kind of paradisaical cruets. The heirs of France take their name from
a "fish"; and have not fishermen given three kings to
Persia and an emperor to Rome ?

But just as many have thus adventitiously arrived at
celebrity, so many others have accidentally fallen into
disrepute. The mackerel can hardly be a proud fish,
recollecting its traditional imputations, nor lobsters go
haughtily. The character of this crustacean in legend is
perhaps worth a passing remark, for it is curious that while
the crab ever holds a place of honour, the lobster should
be always disreputable. Very old engravings show us a

fool astride a lobster; and the significance of that medal
of the Pretender, in which the youthful aspirant is shown
in the arms of a Jesuit who rides a lobster, conveys nothing
to the credit * either of the friar or the fish. Mercury in
his ignobler aspect rides a cray-fish. The porpoise is
popular in the same homely way that the pig is; but the
eel has the worst of characters.

It was a common myth once that the sea held a duplicate of every animal on the earth, and antiquity therefore
was familiar with many marine equivalents for their land-
beasts, even though they could find no better resemblances for the corresponding terrestrial beasts than a
lobster for the " lion," a crab for the " bear," a skate for the
" ox," a dog-fish for the " dog," and an eel for the " wolf."
The names were probably given at first simply to indi-
cate a single point of fancied resemblance, but eventually
some imaginative theorist, seeing so many correspondences
recognised, hit upon the idea of extending the identities
throughout creation. The attempt, however, was a complete failure, and the further enquiry is made, the wider
become the differences between the inhabitants of the
water and the earth. Sailors and fishermen still retain
many of the old names, and popular usage has familiarised
us more or less with the sea-horse—the quaint little
creature, more like a knight on a chess-board than a horse
—sea-lion, sea-bear, sea-cat, sea-eagle, sea-bat, sea-hedge-
hog, sea-leopard, sea-mouse, sea-scorpion, sea-snipe, sea-

* " The imputation upon the legitimacy of the Pretender, conveyed
in the above, was occasioned in a great degree and almost justified by
the pilgrimages and superstitious foolishness of his grandmother,
increased by his mother's choosing St. Francis Xavier as one of her
ecclesiastical patrons, and with her family attributing the birth of the
Prince to his miraculous interference."—*Notes and Queries.*

swallow, sea-parrot, and so forth; while heralds are re-
sponsible for the perpetuation of many amphibious hybrids.
But this tendency to see in the water a reflection of
everything on land is only an instance of human self-
consciousness, for if we were to be just to our seniors in
creation, and more modest, we should call ourselves land-
manatees, our elephants land-whales, and our tigers land-
sharks. As Sir Thos. Browne says—" If we concede that
the animals of one element might bear the names of
those in the other, the watery productions should have
the pre-nomination."

Yet at the bottom of the sea are green fields—such as
Israel walked over when crossing the smitten flood—in
which the small fish take refuge from the greater, just as
the field-mice and birds and insects hide in our own grass.
The Water-baby found at the sea-bottom both meadows
and woods; and Strabo tells us of the flocks of rich fat
tunnies that feed on the acorns of submarine oaks. And
who would doubt their existence who has read how the
prince rides out into mid-ocean to find the casket among
the roots of the tree? Once upon a time, too, if the poet
is to be believed, our birds were all creatures of the sea.
Accident or high spirits took them out of the water into
the moist herbage of the banks, whence they could not
escape, but which was just wet enough to support life.
Their progeny throve there, but their fins, shrivelling,
split up, and the scales, crackling, fell off, and by-and-by
a woolly growth took their place and eventually became
feathers. The under-fins, with which they used to scrape
their way along the sea-floor, became real legs, and thus
the bird grew into existence. This un-Darwinian evolution
was science a few centuries ago, just as it is science now
to understand that the whale once had legs, and roamed

our terrestrial forests—but what a thought! Imagine, in the gloom of a forest, coming upon a whale on legs!

Indeed, it is hardly necessary to go to fable for wonders, for the actual natural world of fishes is a very wilderness of marvels. They come out of the water and migrate in companies across meadows ; they wander along river-banks, hunting for terrestrial insects, unfairly trespassing on the grounds of the lizard and land-bird ; they climb up trees ; are met with travelling along hot and dusty gravel roads under the midday sun ;* have been seen thrown up alive from volcanoes in water that was only two degrees below boiling point.† So the wonders of fish-land, the real world of fishes, is as startling and as marvellous as the fictions of mythology itself, and we need go to no Islands of the Pescadores, nor cruise on the bewitched shores of Calypso, to meet with abundant matter for astonishment.

In character, they range through every variety of temperament, from the gentle carp, that in Java and elsewhere are tamed into the playfulness and familiarity of dormice or caged birds, or the Adonis, "darling of the sea," to the dog-fish, that are cruel and fierce beyond all mammalian comparison. It is true that the Zulus to this day cut flesh out of a living beast, and that other savages do the same ; and in a legend of New Zealand we read how a man used to take occasional snacks out of a pet whale. But what episode is there in all human knowledge more terrible than the manner of the death of those whales which the dog-fish follow for days, and days, and days, living upon them as they go ? Was ever a death more awful, or cruelty more dreadful ? Who, again, has not applauded Trinculo's excellent phrase of an "ancient and fish-like smell," or ever thought of the odour of fish as

---

* Tennant's ' Ceylon.'　　　　　　† Humboldt.

agreeable ? Yet to "smell daintily as a flower or a fish" has been accepted by our forefathers as an allowable simile. One angler says the smelt has a fragrance of lavender ; another that it savours of cucumber ; another that the grayling has the aroma of thyme. St. Ambrose called it the "sweet flower of fishes." The cuttle-fish was supposed with "its sweet odour" to attract fish to it ;* and the whale to obtain its food by opening its mouth, whence issued "so agreeable a scent" that the creatures of the deep gathered together in its jaws to enjoy the fragrant atmosphere. As a general rule, too, the smell of fish cooking is considered rather worse than that of fish raw : yet, says an Athenian enthusiast, "the odour of a cooking conger is so divine that it would make a dead man sniff."

Fish, again, are charged with being voiceless, but how then about the gurnard that pipes, the other that snorts, the diodon that grunts, and the others that drum and whistle and play on Jews' harps ? The legend that they were caught in Egypt by singing to them† is not without its plausibility. "Fishes, though little, have very long ears," is an old Chinese proverb ; and to this day, on the Danube, men hang little bells to their nets to attract the fish. In Japan the tame fish are summoned to dinner by

---

* "And verily all living creatures in the sea love the smell of them exceedingly well, which is the cause that fishers besmeare and anoint their nets with them, to draw and allure fishes thither."—*Historic Devices and Badges.*

† If we may believe Ælian, that most unsophisticated fish, the Thrissa of the Lake Mareotis, "was caught by singing to it, and by the sound of clappers made of shells ;" and so musically inclined was this species, and so sharp in hearing sounds even out of its own element, that, dancing up, it leapt into the net spread for the purpose, giving great and abundant sport.—*Wilkinson's Egypt.*

melodious gongs. In India I have seen them called up out of the muddy depths of the river at Dholpore by the ringing of a hand-bell; and from the abbey in Belgium where the tame carp answer at once to the whistle of the monks who feed them, right away to Otaheite where the chiefs have pet eels which they whistle to the surface, the same belief in the sympathy of fish with musical sounds will on enquiry be found prevailing. "Dull as a mullet" was a Roman proverb, yet the very men who quoted it prided themselves on the docility, sensitiveness to sound, and personal attachments of their favourite mullets. This fish too, as it happens, was consecrated to Diana the huntress, as it was supposed to hunt the sea-hare, and if any one of the Roman divinities was averse to dulness, it was surely the high-spirited Diana.

I am inclined, therefore, to think that the finned folk have been somewhat calumniated. A grudge, it is possible, has been borne against the fish, under the idea that they escaped the Deluge. Thus Whiston, in his philosophical Romance of the Deluge, surmises that the fish living in a cool element were more correct in their lives than the beasts and birds of the sun-lit land, and were therefore spared from the destruction of the primitive world. But it is extremely improbable that the fish did really escape the ruin of the Deluge. If so, it must have been some of the deep-sea forms only, so that envious depreciation of the marine world on this account would seem to be gratuitous. Yet the very word fish itself has come, by some obliquity of reasoning, to signify an object of doubtful character or absurd appearance, and one-half the creatures of the world are treated as a joke by the other half. Beasts are regarded with deference, birds with admiration, but fish are laughed at as absurdities.

Even men of science say that fish life is "silent, monotonous, and joyless," though science itself contradicts
them, as I have already shown; and seriously—if it is
permissible to be serious over a whimsical theory — if
the fish were to have things their own way for a while,
would they not with as much reason (if they argued
with as little sympathy) condemn terrestrial existence as
flat and dull ?   They would pretend that our continents
were accidents of nature; and as for our islands, that
they were merely warts and wens.   The interruptions of
rock and sand, which now prevent their swimming everywhere, would be pronounced ridiculous—good sea all run
to land.   Some scientific fish would get up and point out
what circumscribed lives the things that went on legs had
to lead.   There is neither height above nor depth beneath
in which they can disport; and as for variety of landscape,
the land-folk could make but a poor show as compared
with the water-world.   The limits within which variation
of life-forms are restricted on the earth would afford the
marine critic an excellent point against us, and he could
hit us very hard indeed when he came to ask us if we
had any animated vegetables.   If, again, the fish were to
hold an Exhibition,* they would divide their sections
according to water-spaces and rivers, and not, as man
does, according to the geography of dry land ; while their
exhibits would possess such a thrilling interest for humanity
as nothing could surpass, except that apocalyptic solution
of all the world's mysteries at the Last Day—when the sea
shall give up its dead.

* See Appendix to Handbook.

CHAPTER II.

What Pantagruel saw in Lantern-land—The Greek Naturalists—The dignity of the Fish Myth, and of Zoological Mythology in general — Fish in the Solar Myth — Fish-version of Reineke Fuchs—Vishnu's Fish-Avatar—The Phallical Fish—The Philanthropic Dolphin, a Hellenic creation—The Cosmopolitan Turtle Myth—Purely fanciful Fishes—The Stay-ship and others — Sea Monsters, their persistence in popular belief—Lawrens Andrewe, "hys Fisshes."

WHEN Pantagruel was on his travels, he came, he tells us, "into the country of Tapestry, and saw the Mediterranean Sea open to the right and left down to the very bottom : just as the Red Sea very fairly left its bed at the Arabian gulf, to make a lane for the Jews, when they left Egypt. There I found Triton winding his silver shell instead of a horn, and also Glaucus, Proteus, Nereus, and a thousand other godlings and sea monsters. I also saw an infinite number of fish of all kinds, dancing, flying, vaulting, fighting, eating, breathing, hitting, shoving, spawning, fishing, skirmishing, lying in ambuscade, making truces, cheapening, bargaining, swearing, and sporting. In a blind corner I saw Aristotle holding a lantern, in the posture in which the hermit uses to be drawn near St. Christopher, watching, prying, thinking, and setting everything down in writing."

But if Aristotle had not taken his lantern into the depths of nature, the world for some centuries would have been more ignorant and superstitious than it was, and we

owe to him and to Strabo and Oppian, Ælian and Pliny—
those brave old thinkers who, in spite of the shoals of error
and the fogs of myth, tried their hardest to keep the ship's
head straight for the glimmering beacon-light of Truth—
more than we can ever repay. For though the world has
grown beyond their facts, and modern science has sifted
their knowledge through and through — indeed, I should
like to see a fine imposed upon those writers who still
persist in larding their lean pages with quotations from
them, and imprisonment without the option of a fine
upon all who call Pliny "quaint" — yet their works, the
Pyramids of old-world thought, abound in significances
that can never lose their interest. Zoological mythology
is no whimsical study. It reaches out with arms of
astronomical power to the beginnings of time, demonstrates
the continuity of human intelligence, and proves the evolution of modern creeds.

And since in the beginning there were only Light and
Water, the eldest of zoological myths is the Fish-myth.
Asia believes the earth to have been saved by a fish
and to be supported on a tortoise ; Polynesia, that it was
brought up, a fish itself, on a fish-hook, out of the primæval
ocean ; America, that a turtle, the sole tenant of the waste
of waters, dived for it into the depths of diluvian chaos.
Among the most ancient of Syrian divinities is the fish-
form ; it is found among the remoter antiquities of Egypt ;
primitive Europe saw gods in its fish. Thus gradually,
down through the ages, the same symbol was passed on
from nation to nation, and the sea, from its mystery, its
acknowledged seniority, claimed conspicuous honours in
each Pantheon, until, reaching historic times, we find the
Greeks—borrowing they knew not whence— perpetuating
the original myth, and adding to it as only the subtle

Greek spirit could. And how bright their sea-life was, with its goddesses that sailed about in shells, and gods that rode on dolphins ; when mariners saw chariots drawn by sea-horses, hurrying along to scenes of submarine revelry, and heard in the bays the music bubbling up from the sea-kings' palaces ! In the beautiful Greek waters were troops of happy people, and it seems no hard fate for Pompilus or for Nais, or any of the other men or women, who for their misdemeanours were condemned to the livery of scales, to have been banished in the Golden Age of fishes from the solid earth to the subaqueous regions where Neptune held his glad court, and Amphitrite her revels. And then came those grand old thinking men, trying, out of a chaos of superstitions to deduce scientific order, and yet preserving for us in their pages all those credulities which now enable us to retrace the paths of human thought, and locate the sources of human beliefs.

In the Solar Myth the fish has been made, like every-thing else, to play a prominent part : the fair-haired and silvery moon, in the ocean of night, is the little gold-fish and the little silver-fish which announces the rainy season, the autumn, the deluge ; out of the cloudy, nocturnal or wintry ocean comes forth the sun, the pearl lost in the sea, which the gold or silver fish brings out. The little gold-fish and the luminous pike, like the moon, expands or contracts, and in this form, as expanding or contracting, the god Vishnu or Hari (which means fair-haired or golden) refers now to the sun, now to the moon, Vishnu having taken the form of the gold-fish. But the commixture of accidental coincidences and incongruous objects which go to make up the myth that Gubernatis sets forth in its most bewildering aspect, has in itself material for volumes, and it is enough here to say, that those who go to any work on the subject will be surprised to find how large a space the fishes fill in this mythological maze. Indra, who had to hide in the waters ; Adrika, the fish-nymph, who became the mother of Matsyas, the king of the fishes ; the Puranic fishes, symbolical and natural ; the fishes of the Eddas, with the scaly transformations of Andvarri and Loki ; the porpoises that draw the golden chariot ; the Russian whale that swallows the fleet, or the Hindoo one that swallows the monkey-god ; the brown pike that is really the devil and hopes to eat the hero ; the shark that devours the princess ; the phallical pike with the golden fins ; the fish that helps the lazy baker's son ; the eels with all their disreputable significances ; the fishes that laugh ; the dolphins that find Ivan's ring ; the turbulent perch, and the golden carp into which Vishnu turns himself ; all combine with donkeys and blackbirds, bull-moons and fish-moons, rainclouds, twilights, and thunderbolts, bamboos and hares, luminous and "diabolical," into a mythical cycle of fishes, or, as the master calls it, "their epic exploit," that ought, if anything can, to give the reader a broader sense of the possibilities of fish than he probably ever expected to entertain.

Two of the myths I have referred to will bear more than a passing notice, for the story of the turbulent perch shows a singular affinity in its scheme to "Reynard the Fox," while the fish transformations of Vishnu form an important item of piscine mythology. The jorsh, or little perch, makes itself such a public enemy, that it is called before the royal tribunal, and the bream, and the herring, and the sturgeon all give evidence of the evil conduct of the perch. Judgment of death is accordingly passed upon it, and the crayfish seals the warrant with its claw. But the jorsh rails violently against what it calls the conspiracy against it, spits at the judge and, jumping out of the dock, escapes. He continues his misdemeanours, and fish after fish is sent to bring him again to the bar. He cleverly gets the better of the messengers, but at last comes and demands a judgment from God. This is permitted, and the jorsh having got into a net, manages to wriggle out again, and is thereupon acquitted, and straightway recommences to annoy all his neighbours worse than ever. This myth, from its resemblance to *Reineke Fuchs*, is obviously an important one in the Thier-epos upon which comparative mythologists work; while the other, that of Vishnu's fish-incarnation, has a dignity of its own, apart from its possible lunar interpretation, as an episode of one of the great religious epics of Asia. The god had become a small fish, and in this form went to Menu, praying for his protection against the larger creatures of the water. The sage, in pity, put the little thing into a water-jar; but in a single night it grew large enough to fill the jar, so Menu put it into a pond. Here the same increase was repeated, and so the fish was taken to the Ganges; but the river soon proved all too restricted for the expanding monster, and it was therefore conveyed to the Sea. Upon this the god made himself known, and warned the sage that in seven days the earth would be overwhelmed by a Flood; but, said the fish, " You must build a ship, and enter it, with seven sages, with a pair of every kind of living thing, and with the seeds of all kinds of plants;" and it promised, when the flood subsided, to come and tell the inmates of the ark. In due time, accordingly, the god, still in the fish shape, appeared, and Menu, making a rope fast to the horn of the fish, was towed to Naubandha, and there the ark rested upon the mountain peak. The Diluvian Legend, therefore, is older than the inspiration of Moses, and the Biblical narrative of Noah's arrangements had been anticipated by some centuries.

In the later myths—those, for instance, of Greece and Rome—though they, too, reach back by similarities both of design and detail to a distant past, fishes retain their prominence. The distant, mystical ocean was then an object of awful reverence. The nearer seas were governed by powerful but kindly divinities. But both alike were populous with strange fishes, and romantic with legends.

The chief water-myth was that of Aphrodite. Sometimes she springs, a perfect goddess, from the sea itself; at others fish roll on to the shore an egg, from which, a dove brooding on it, the mother of Love is born. Later on, she and her son Eros, to escape the tumult of giant-beleaguered Olympus, hide in the Euphrates in the form of fish; and yet again we find the goddess taking the starry Pisces under her protection. So, too, Athor, the Egyptian Venus, had been a fish; and so, too, Derceto, the Syrian love-nymph. In the Puranic legend a fish receives the love-god, and assists him to espouse Maya.

In the limited space of a handbook—even if it were proper to its object—it would be impossible to enumerate all the fish-myths of the so-called classical period, and I will therefore select only those that seem to me typical of the four classes into which the whole group themselves.

As essentially Greek in brightness of conception is the myth of the philanthropic dolphin. It was pre-eminently the friend of man, and a creature of gladness. Whenever needed it was present, and the stories of its lending itself as the vehicle of gods and nymphs, poets and schoolboys, are too numerous for recapitulation.* Endowed by tradition with perfectly super-cetaceous virtues, it was accepted by all, mariner and landsman alike, as an amiable ally. The scientific mythologist, as may easily be imagined, has made much of the dolphin, but ingenuity can never get more out of the old myth than that the natural habits of this animal endeared it in the past to all sea-goers, just as they have endeared it to those of the present. Eros, therefore, the blithest of gods, rides on a dolphin—Amphitrite has one for a guardian—and when out a merry-making all the jolly sea-magnates have dolphins tumbling about them. They brought Hesiod's body to shore ; and Ulysses, in gratitude for their saving Telemachus, wore their effigy upon both signet-ring and shield. All fish are benign in fairy tale, but the sum of their united amiabilities hardly equals the services conferred in myth and legend by the dolphin upon the human race. Well does the swift cetacean deserve its place among the stars.

In contradistinction to the dolphin, a purely Hellenic creation, we may place the world-wide, cosmopolitan, turtle. Though a creature to laugh over when we see it creeping stealthily about on tiptoe, as if it were abroad for the purpose of picking pockets, it has a very notable place in myth, for it was almost universally reverenced. The East believes that the world rests upon a tortoise, which rests upon nothing—and what a grand old testacean it is, this Vedic turtle,

---

* "They loved music, especially of the 'hydraulic sort' (whatever that sort may have been), and they were easily tamed, and fondly attached to men. Pliny says he should never end all the stories he knows of the obliging behaviour of dolphins, who allowed children to ride on their backs. One of them—as attested by Mæcenas and Fabianus—in the reign of Augustus, carried a boy every morning to school, and when the lad died the dolphin pined away waiting for him on the shore, and at last expired of grief."—*Frances P. Cobbe.*

standing simply on its own dignity, and yet upholding upon
its Atlantic carapace all the burdens of the round world and
them that dwell therein! Here is a subject for Walt
Whitman himself, the self-sufficient, democratic, thewy-and-
sinewy, double-sexed, bully-for-you, old tortoise. More
power to your shell, sir! We creeping things take off our
hats to you, testudinous ancient. And how splendidly
the deliberate thing looms out of Hindoo myth as the hereditary foe of the mystical elephant, the Darkness!* The
Red Indian to this day says that in the beginning of
things there was nothing but a tortoise. It brooded upon
space : covered Chaos as with a lid. But after a while it
woke up : its solitary existence was irksome to it, and it
sank splendidly into the abysmal depths ; and lo ! when it
re-emerged, there was the terrestrial globe upon its back !
For something to do, it had fished up our earth from its
depths in the protoplasmic liquids, and, rather than be idle, it
still keeps on holding it up. But some day it will sink again,
and then will come the End—with Ragnarok and Arma-
geddon. In Greek and Roman fancies the tortoise hardly
fares so well. It is the form to which a bright nymph, who
had jested at the nuptials of Zeus and Heré, was turned
into by Mercury ; and ridicule falls upon the greatest of the
Greeks when a tortoise falls upon his head. Yet they, too,

---

* " As the elephant and tortoise both frequent the shores of the same
lake, they mutually annoy each other, renewing and maintaining in
mythical zoology the strife which exists between the two mythical
brothers who fight with each other for the kingdom of the heavens,
either in the form of twilights or of equinoxes, or of sun and moon.
In the particular struggle between the tortoise and the elephant,
terminated by the bird Garuda, who carries them both up into the
air in order to devour them, the tortoise and elephant seem, however,
especially to personify the two twilights of the day, and the two twilights
of the year."—*Gubernatis.*

knew of the tradition of the world-supporting thing, and did reverence to it. And so, from East to West, from antiquity to to-day, the creature vast, ponderous, inert, has commanded, and commands the homage of men.

As a third type of myth—the fanciful without any latent significance — the remora or sucking-fish, may be cited. In modern times it has been used to illustrate the power of technical trivialities to retard a lawsuit, but antiquity believed it had the power of arresting a ship under full sail by attaching its tail-end to a rock, and its head-end to the keel of a passing vessel—

> " The lazy Remora's inhaling lips,
> Hung on the keel, retard the struggling ships."

In the Natural History of the period we read that "there is a little fish, keeping ordinarie about rockes, named Echeneis. It is thought that if it settle and sticke to the keel of a ship under water, the ship goeth the slower by that means, wherefore it is called the 'stay-ship.'" Now, Pliny is here cautious enough, and attributes no more to the remora than is actually the property of barnacles when in number. But popular fancy outran fact, and a single remora four inches long was supposed to have held back Antony's flag-ship in the sea-fight off Actium. Periander also among others declared himself the victim of a similar accident,* and the fiction flourished, thanks

---

* It is of this incident that Pantagruel makes fun :—

" I saw a remora, a little fish called echineis by the Greeks, and near it a tall ship, that did not get ahead an inch, though she was in the offing with top and top-gallants spread before the wind. I am somewhat inclined to believe, that 'twas the very identical ship in which Periander the tyrant happened to be, when it was stopt by such a little fish in spite of wind and tide."—*Rabelais.*

chiefly to poets and heralds, till a couple of centuries ago.

> " The sucking-fish, with secret chains
> Clung to the keel, the swiftest ship detains."

Of late years, of course, this fancy has been exploded, and instead of being the terrible thing antiquity thought it, the remora is really like the little street boy who gets on to the step of the omnibus when the conductor is not looking, and gets a penny ride for nothing. For the fish attaches itself to the shark and others, merely, it would seem, for the luxury of cheap travelling. Yet knowing this, what are we to say of Mr. Francis Holmwood's astounding discovery at Zanzibar of the "sucking-fish" that is used to catch sharks and crocodiles ? Here, at any rate, are his own words, as quoted from the "Exhibition Catalogue," p. 382 :—

"Young chazo (sucking-fish) being secured, a ring or hoop of iron is let into the tails ; they are then kept in a small canoe, the water in which is changed from time to time. They are fed sparingly with pieces of meat and fish, and, if they survive the confinement, soon become used to captivity and to being handled. When they have reached two or three pounds in weight, they are strong enough for use, and are taken out for trial. A line is fastened to the iron hoop, which has become embedded in a firm growth, and on sighting a tortoise or turtle, the chaze is put overboard. It has to be prevented from affixing itself to the canoe, and then it soon makes for the nearest floating object, to which it instantly adheres, and generally allows itself to be drawn with its prey towards the boats. Should it prove too timid to stand this treatment it is discarded as worthless, but if it will hold on, it soon gets bold enough to retain its hold until taken into the boat, when it is at once detached from the prize by being drawn off sideways, and being returned to its tank is at once fed. They are said soon to learn what is required of them, and it is reported that they have been trained to catch sharks. When in Madagascar some years ago, I was told that the "Tarundu," which the fish is there called, had been trained to catch crocodiles, numbers of which infested the rivers and, as I observed, came down to the neighbourhood of the fishing villages on the coast, without being affected by the salt water. I hope to forward a specimen of this interesting fish before the close of the Exhibition."

An official footnote to this passage is as follows:—" Up to the time of going to press with the Second Edition, this exhibit had not arrived." And if any confidence is ever to be reposed in modern science as opposed to ancient fancy, let us hope this terrific creature never *will* arrive.

In this class of merely fanciful creatures may be also noticed the Pompilus, the sailor's pilot-fish, which was supposed to guide mariners to their destinations, and, having seen them safely into harbour, to go back to look for another job, for Apollo, it is said, changed a fisherman (named Pompilus), who had crossed him in his loves, into this fish, and condemned him for all eternity to the task of gratuitous pilotage. The whale, again, was said to be attended by the "musculus," a little fish that swam in front of Behemoth and warned him off the shoals on which he might have otherwise run aground. This legend reappears in the Pentameron, where the whale that has lost its way is told to go and get "the sea-mouse" to pilot it.

As the fourth class of zoological myths, may be grouped the non-existent sea-monsters—

> " Most ugly shapes and horrible aspects,
>   Such as Dame Nature selfe mote feare to see,
>   Or shamed, that ever should so fowle defects
>   From her most cunning hand escaped bee ;
>   All dreadfull pourtraicts of deformitee :
>   Spring-headed Hydres ; and sea-shouldring whales :
>   Great whirlpooles, which all fishes make to flee ;
>   Bright scolopendraes arm'd with silver scales ;
>   Mighty monoceres with immeasured tayles."

Græco-Roman literature abounds with them, especially such as were hybrids between men and fish, or between

terrestrial and marine animals, and their counterparts
are to be found in the folk-lore* of every coast-dwelling
people at the present day. I will only notice here the
Scylla-myth. Her form is very variously described, but
the most familiar acceptation is that which combines the
woman, dog, and fish. She gives her name to the dreadful Scyllidæ of science, one of which, the black-mouthed
dog-fish, is known to Italian fishermen as the "Bocca
d'Inferno "—

> " As a shark and dogfish wait
>   Under an Atlantic isle
>   For the negro-ship whose freight
>   Is the theme of their debate,
>   Wrinkling their red gills the while."

Yet they eat it, and its even more appalling relative, the
Rough Hound—converting these terrors of the sea into a
very palatable soup

With the growth of knowledge and the extension of
navigation, the Hellenic monstrosities, themselves the re-
production of still more ancient myths, became gradually
discredited ; but travellers, and those who lived by catering
to the human love of the marvellous, were not behindhand
in replacing them with others better suited to contemporary
taste and sentiment. Among the more impossible monstrosities that the Middle Ages possessed, the sea-bishop,
that had a shark's head, crocodile's claws, and goat's legs,
deserved all the eminence it attained ; while, not far behind
it, came the monk-fish, a tolerably good caricature of a
friar, constructed by the showmen of the day out of portions
of different fish, but nevertheless as thoroughly believed in
by the fair-frequenting public as any pig-faced lady of
modern times. This credulity as to "fish-like monsters "

* See Chapter VII.

suggests to Trinculo making a fortune out of Caliban, whom he has mistaken for a sea-creature. "Were I in England now, and had but this fish painted, not a holiday fool there but would give a piece of silver : there would this monster make a man ; any strange beast there makes a man." We still have the monk-fish, and though the face might pass for a malignant travesty of the human countenance, there are none of the monkish habiliments which made the old-world monster so attractive to the peep-show public. Indeed, the other name of the monk is the "angel-fish," from the wing-like fins that spread out on either side its demoniacal countenance.

Still later, and coming down to England itself, three centuries ago we find popular ichthyology still largely concerned with non-existent forms, as the following from the work of Lawrens Andrewe, on "the fishes moste knowen," will show :—The eel is of no sex ; the Ahuna, when "in peryl of dethe be other fisshes," makes himself as round as a bowl and puts his head in his belly and eats a bit of himself, "rather than the other fisshes sholde ete him hole and all." The balæna, a large merwoman, puts her young in her mouth in rough weather ; the cray-fish eats oysters by waiting till the mollusc opens its shells, and then throwing stones in to prevent it shutting up again ; the caucius is most difficult to net, because when it sees the meshes settling on it, it sticks its head in the mud and the net slips over the tail ; the whale is caught by ships coming round it with bands and amusing it with music till it is speared ; the phoca kills its wife when it is tired of her, and gets another ; the halata has the power of taking her young out before they are born, and putting them back again ; the pike is begotten by the west wind ; the musculus is the herald of balæna, but the orchun

is its deadliest enemy, for it pelts it with stones till it kills
it ; the serra races with ships, and, if it gets the worst of
it, cuts the vessels through with its fins and eats the crew,
but is not to be mistaken for the scylla, which is " faced
and handed lyke a gentylwoman, but it hath a wyde
mouth and ferfull tethe ; " the way to escape the siren
when met with, is to throw her an empty barrel or two to
play with ; the sturgeon has no mouth, and grows fat on
east winds."

Or take again the ' Old English Miscellany,' with its
account of the Cetegrande :—" It is the largest of all fish,
and looks like an island when afloat. When hungry, it
gapes, and out comes a sweet scent, by which numbers of
fishes are drawn into its mouth.

" MORAL : The Devil is like the Whale ; he tempts men
to follow their sinful lusts, and in return they find ruin."

CHAPTER III.

FISHES IN RELIGION.

Primitive Fish-Divinities—and Greco-Roman—Fish-spirits and Genii—
Patron Saints — Sacred fishes — Fish-totems — Fish not eaten
because sacred—Fish sacred because not eatable—Fish both sacred
and eaten—Putting off the Gods with the Worst fish—Magnifying
them with the Best—Religious Fish-legends, Savage, Hindoo,
Buddhist, Mahomedan—Fish as Food—Christian Legends—Holy
Church perpetuating the Heathen Worship of Venus in Lent—Fish
a Christian Symbol.

"WHEN Kareya made all things that have breath, he first
made the fishes in the Big Water." So say the Red
Indians, and the legend goes on, curiously enough, to tell
how Kareya, in a dog-in-the-manger spirit, kept the fish
(they were salmon) to himself, but how man, with the help
of the coyote, the prairie-jackal, outwitted the Creator, and
got the salmon up stream. Does this point to an artificial
system of fish-ladders being known to the primitive savage?
At any rate, it authenticates the dignity of fish in the
cosmogony of the aboriginal American. But, as older
even than this antiquity, we must accept the Polynesian
theory of creation. In this the Creator is himself half a
fish. That is to say, from the head to the feet, the left
side of the body is fish. Coming down, however, to more
recent mythologies, we find the senior of the gods of
Olympus, the ever-youthful Eros, is a fish, and his so-called
"mother" a fish also. We may note, too, that Jupiter
never asserted control over Neptune. On the sea-shore,

near Delphi, sate a priest who delivered his oracles according to the fish that his visitors saw in the waters below.
At the present day, if we go to the far North, we find the
elements under the control of the Spirits of the Sea,
irrespective of the powers of the land.

That the Ocean appealed very strongly to the natural
reverence of humanity is thus abundantly in evidence, and
we find fish, therefore, occupying a very conspicuous place
in the world's beliefs. And apart from the creative powers
identified with fish and the divinities that held marine
dominion, the creatures of the water could claim the
special tutelage of Venus (under all her varying names), of
Apollo Opsophagus, and of Artemis, the guardian goddess
of fresh waters. In the Dagon form they found gods of
their own natural order in many lands, and in Scandinavia
knew Odin the All-father as a fish. The number of
deities, primitive and classical, that have at one time or
another assumed the piscine incarnation is very great, and
ranges from Vishnu, the Hindoo Jehovah, to Loki, the
Norseman's Mercury.

Of subordinate fish-spirits there is a still larger number ;
which are graduated from the New Zealander's Tangaroo,
through the Genii of the Lake and the Gulnares of the
Sea, to the Arnarkuagsak and Ingnersuaks of the Arctic
regions, and thereafter dwindle away into mere maritime
goblins, Nöks and Soetrolds, Grim and Fosse-grim, that
are only a superior sort of " Davy Jones."

In mediæval times the fish found, too, several Patron
Saints. St. Peter of course stands at the head, as a fisherman himself, and actor in the fish-miracles * of Holy Writ,

* It is one of these, the finding of the tribute-money, that gives the
haddock,
         " A superstitious dainty, Peter's fish,"
its legendary celebrity, the monks averring that it was a haddock

and to this day the Company of the Fishmongers bear
the crossed keys of the saint on their arms. That St.
Peter's tutelage of fishes and his fief of fisheries was no
empty assertion of the Church, may be understood from
the fact that the Abbot of St. Peter's, Westminster,
claimed all the salmon caught in the Thames, on the
ground that the Saint had granted the same to him
when he consecrated the Church. After St. Peter came
St. Anthony (who preached to the fishes with such effect),
St. Christopher, St. Zeno, and St. Andrew of Scotland.

St. Anthony, as is well known, the patron saint of
animals of all kinds, utilised his power over fishes in a very
meritorious manner, by calling them up from the sea to
listen to his preaching, and thus put to shame some stiff-
necked heretics of Rimini who refused to listen to his
pious counsels. A delightful woodcut in an old chap-
book depicts the saint, in the attitude of exhortation,
addressing a company of fishes, that poke long goose-like
necks out of the water to listen to him, while on the bank
—expressing by their gestures their surprise at the miracle
and, perhaps, foreshowing also their own approaching con-
version—stand in file the stubborn scorners of his teaching.

That St. Christopher was always a patron saint of fishermen is certain, but for what reason seems somewhat ob-
scure. He certainly lived on the river-side, for, so the
legend says, he earned his living by carrying people across

(a sea-water fish) that the saint caught in the fresh-water lake of
Genesaret. This of course only adds another miracle to the original
episode. In a miracle which Jesus worked, and of which, though
Holy Writ is silent the Koran preserves the tradition, there descended
from Heaven a red table upon which were seven loaves and seven
fishes, and the latter tasted at each mouthful of a different Paradisaical
delicacy. When all had feasted to their heart's content, Jesus restored
the fishes to life.

the water, but nothing is said of his having been an enthusiastic angler. The inference no doubt was that, as no man
could be expected to live all his life by the side of a run-
ning stream, especially with long intervals of idleness in his
days, without angling, the saint eked out his income, and
passed his time, by fishing. It was in that notable passage
of the river, when he carried the child-Christ across, that he
caught the John Dory, a sea-water fish, and left the marks of
the pinch which he gave it to be handed down *in memoriam*
to the Dory's posterity. This fish, by the way, had a certain
classical sanctity as being called Zeus, and Aristotle has a
"sacred fish," the Anthias, which, from his description of
its habits, has been conjectured to be the John Dory. It
was also called Faber, "the blacksmith," and so under the
protection of Hephaistos, Mulciber, or Vulcan. Again, the
Apah, or king-fish, * is a native of the eastern seas, and it
is not a little singular that, by a people so distant and
secluded as the Japanese, this fish (originally included in
the genus Zeus) should also be regarded as devoted to the
Deity, and the only one that is so. The Apah is by them
termed Tai, and is esteemed as the peculiar emblem of
happiness, because it is sacred to Jebis or Neptune.

St. Zeno was an enthusiastic angler, and therefore worked
for, and earned, his position as a patron saint. He was
probably an advocate of preserving waters. To this list I
have added the patron saint of Scotland, for we read in
the adventures of the "Seven Champions of Christendom,"
how, on the fourth day, by the emperor's appointment,
the worthy knight St. Andrew of Scotland obtained the
honour to be the chief challenger for the tournament, "and
how his tent was framed to represent a ship swimming
upon the waves of the sea, environed by dolphins, tritons,

* Yarrell.

and many strangely-contrived mermaids ; and upon the top thereof stood the picture of Neptune the god of the sea." That a Christian knight, already well assured of canonisation, should have fought under such pagan tutelage, is enough to scandalise the Sabbatarian North. But such are the facts.

St. Benedict of Ramsey Mere claims also a fraction of the patronage, as also does St. Benignus, who may be seen at Glastonbury with his fish at his feet. Shellfish may fairly be said to have a patron saint all to themselves in St. James of Spain, and the crustaceans one in St. Xavier.

Among sacred fish, less well known, are " the Sheikh " and " the Prophet's fish." Says the Arabic legend :—

" A Sicilian cast a hook into the Mediterranean and caught a fish about a span long. Under its right ear were the words, ' There is no God but the God,' and behind it the word ' Muhammad,' and under its left ear ' The Apostle of God.' "

And again :—

" A fish called the Jewish Shaikh has a long white beard and a body as large as a calf, but in the shape of a frog, and hairy like a cow. It is called the Shaikh because it comes out of the sea on Saturday and remains there until sundown on Sunday."

An analogy to this Sabbath-observing fish is to be found in the commentators on the Koran, where we are told that the fish, in order to tempt the Hebrews, used to come up to the camp on Saturday mornings, and provoke the poor wanderers to catch them. And the Hebrews, thinking to avoid sin, went out and dammed up the channel, and then ate the fish on the next day. But as there was little difference in the matter of " working on the Sabbath " between fishing and dam-building, they were very properly punished· for this violation of the Day of Rest by being all turned into apes.

Totemism, the system of tribal emblems—" medicine animals " and " clan-animals "—brings into the category of sacred fish another class of great interest, namely those which have been selected by primitive clans as their tutelary genii.*   Thus the Pike, Trout, and Sturgeon are among the totems of Red Indian tribes.   There are Fish-tribes of both Africans and Australians.   Among the Fijians are Eels, Crabs, and Sharks.   These individual fishes, thus chosen as the tribal badge, are held sacred by those who have adopted them.   They are called the progenitors of the tribe, and are never eaten, nor, if possible, even molested.   Among the Wakerewé (of Africa) it is believed that the fish of a neighbouring lake are their special ministers and creatures, and are therefore under their protection.   If a fish-hawk so much as touches one, it dies in the very act.   With another African race the drum-head fish is taboo, and its teeth, rattled in the fetich-man's gourd, give forth Delphic utterances.

Going back to the past again, we find fish arriving at sanctity by previous uncleanness, and cities taking their totems, so to speak, from the polluted creatures which in the lapse of time they came to worship.   When Isis was collecting the remains of the body of Osiris, she found a portion missing, and discovering that the fish had eaten it, the three species found in the river at that part were forbidden to be eaten by the people of the neighbourhood. The Egyptians in general, says Plutarch, do not absta. from all fish, but some from one sort and some from another.   Thus the Oxyrhinchites will not touch any fish taken by a hook, for as they pay special deference to the oxyrhinchus, from which they take their name, they are afraid the hook may be defiled by having, at some time or

* See also Chap. VII.

other, been employed in catching their favourite fish. If
one of this kind were found in a net full of others, the
whole draught was set at liberty rather than take captive a
single oxyrhinchus. The people of Syene, again, regarded
the phagrus as the herald of the rising Nile, and as such
abstained from it. This eel gave its name to Phagriopolis,
another to Latapolis, while Elephantine venerated the
mæotis, a silurian. But fishes proper are of frequent
occurrence in Egyptian sculpture, and among the articles
placed with the dead were very often small effigies in metal
and clay of the fish-form; while dead fish of the sacred
species were buried with as much ceremony as the cats,
ibises, crocodiles, and other creatures that the Children of
the Pharaohs worshipped.

These Egyptian fish were not of course totems in the
proper sense; for the primitive man performs an act of
positive sacrifice when he devotes to the religious tribal
idea the best fish of the waters, and thenceforward abstains
from eating them, whereas the Egyptians shabbily denied
themselves only the refuse. They made that sacred which
they could not eat. For it is an interesting fact that all
the evidence we have on the point strongly tends to the
suspicion that the pagan gods were put off by the priests
with the very worst of the fish. If a species was poisonous,
or belonged to a class that was generally unwholesome, it
was declared "sacred"; the Church thus exerting its influence to prevent only that being eaten which was already,
in their opinion, unfit for food. In the Mosaic prohibitions
we find that fish without scales and fins were unclean, the
reason probably being that the law-giver had just come up
from Egypt, where the scaleless fish were taboo in consequence of their notorious unwholesomeness. Out of the
six species venerated by the ancient Egyptians, two were

quite unfit for food and a third not worth the eating. The identity of the remainder has never been established, but the chances are that they belonged to sorts that no Egyptian would have eaten even if it had been permitted.

This process of hygienic selection does not extend, obviously, to the rest of the animal world, and yet the theory, if tested with beasts and birds, would, I venture to think, be found more widely applicable than might be expected. Another reason for forbidding certain animals as food was of course their being more useful in other ways; but as this does not concern fish (whose only uses are after death), it appears to me that the only system on which the priests of the oldest times—the thinking men of the community—distributed the honours of consecration among the finny tribes was selection by common sense.

I have now referred to fish that were not eaten because they were sacred, and to fish that were sacred because they were not eatable. There still, however, remains the fish which were both sacred and eaten. Leaving the Græco-Roman affectation of consecration out of the question, we find in India, where the fish holds a place of the highest importance in the religious system, a fish diet universal. The Ruhoo, bearing on its back three goddesses, personifies the junction of the three sacred rivers at Prayaga,* "the confluence," one of the holiest spots in India, where the Ganges and the Jumna combine with the mystic Saraswati that is supposed to flow underground to meet them here. Yet this fish is one of the staples of the food of a large proportion of the citizens of Prayaga. As a solitary fish, Vishnu filled the primæval ocean, and as a fish he rescued the Ark from the Deluge.

* Allahabad.

" In the whole world of creation,
None were seen but these seven sages, Manu and the Fish.
Years on years, and still unwearied, drew this Fish the bark
    along,
Till at length it came where reared Himavan its loftiest peak ;
There at length they came, and smiling, thus the Fish addressed the
    Sage :
' Bind now thy stately vessel to the peak Himavan !'
At the Fish's mandate, quickly to the peak of Himavan
Bound the Sage his bark ; and even to this day that loftiest peak
Bears the name Naubandha."

As a fish, Brahma instructed Manu in all wisdom. It
was a fish that saved Kama, the love-god, and restored him
to the earth, yielding its own life for his. Varuna, the
genius of the waters, is the special protector of the fish
therein. Yet, as I have said, the whole country is ichthyophagous. Were it not that other facts forbid it, we might
whimsically detect in this impartial sanctity, combined with
impartial consumption, a vein of reasoning analogous to
that which leads the Polynesian to enrol all his best fish
in his myths and then to eat them. That which he mag-
nifies alive he canonises dead, thus adding to the three
aspects of the pious-economic fish-myth a fourth, of a
people who deify fishes out of gratitude to excellence, and
call those most sacred which are the best eating.

Religious fish-legends next concern us. They are a
literature in themselves. The Hindoo and the primitive I
have already touched on. In the Buddhist Birth-stories,
the oldest of folk-lore extant, the Teacher finds frequent
subject for parable and moral in the finned things of the
river. The love-sick monk in a previous existence was a
fish, and his uxorious enthusiasm carried him into a net,
and Buddha, passing along, found him about to be fried,
and restored him to the water, telling him to go and
sin no more. It was by her compassion to a fish that

Well-born arrives at her rewards, and from the story of the talkative tortoise that Lord Buddha admonished the loquacious king.

In Mahomedan tradition there is much fish-lore of the most curious kind, and commentators on the Koran vie with the Talmudists in the grotesqueness of invention. As a single example, I will take "The fish of Moses and Joshua," which, read irreverently, is really only a delightful explanation of flat-fish having so much more meat on one side than the other. Moses and Joshua ate the other half. The legend runs thus:—

"Moses was asked who was the most knowing of men, to which he answered, 'I'; whereupon God blamed him for this, because he did not refer the knowledge thereof to Him. And God said unto him by revelation, 'Verily I have a servant at the place where the two seas meet, and he is more knowing than thou.' Moses said, 'O my Lord, and how shall I meet him?' He answered, 'Thou shalt take a fish, and put it into a measuring vessel, and where thou shalt lose the fish, there is he.' So he took a fish, and put it into a vessel. Then he departed, and Joshua the son of Nun departed with him, until they came to a rock, where they laid down their heads and slept. And the fish became agitated in the vessel, and escaped from it and fell into the sea, and it made its way in the sea by a hollow passage, God withholding the water from the fish so that it became like a vault over it, and when Moses' companion awoke, he forgot to inform him of the fish."

But on their way they remembered it, and turned back to find it, and, coming to the rock again, there they met the man who was wiser than Moses. Now the question arose, What was the fish? and the answer was supplied by Hamed of Andalusia, who states that he saw in the Mediterranean "the fish of Moses and Joshua":—

"It is of the breed of that fried fish a half of which Moses and Joshua ate and the other half God revived. It is about a span long. On its one side it has bristles and its belly is covered with a thin skin.

It has but one eye and half a head. Looking at it on one side you would deem it dead, but the other side is perfect in all its parts. The people consider it as a good augury, and the Jews pay a large sum for it and carry it away to distant places."

The Koran allows the faithful to fish in the sea when on pilgrimage (but not to hunt game by the way), and sea-fish were specially permitted as food. At first they were unlawful, as the name of Allah frequently could not be pronounced over them before they died; but, to remedy this, Mahomed, blessing a knife, cast it into the sea, whereby all the fish were blessed, and had their throats cut before they were brought on shore. "The large openings behind the gills are the wounds thus miraculously made without killing the fish." Another legend on the same subject says that Abraham, having sacrificed the ram instead of Isaac, threw away the knife into the stream that flowed near the altar, and accidentally struck a fish. "Fishes therefore are the only animals eaten by Mahomedans without previously having their throats cut."

By the Christian religion the consumption of fish is directly encouraged, for, apart from the general precedent afforded by the miracles in Holy Writ, the Church specially enjoins the diet; and this, too, on such a scale that in the time of Queen Elizabeth, the annual "fish days" * were 145 in number. Among the annual Church

---

* The chief were the forty days of Lent; the Ember-days at the four seasons, being the Wednesday, Friday, and Saturday after the first Sunday in Lent; the feast of Pentecost (Whitsuntide); September 14; December 13; the three Rogation-days, being the Monday, Tuesday, and Wednesday before Holy Thursday; and all the Fridays in the year, except Christmas-day when it falls on a Friday. Even after the Reformation the number of fish-days continued large, about 1596-7 those observed by the household of Queen Elizabeth being only some thirty-seven days short of half the year.

disbursements up to the end of the 16th century were herrings, "red and white," to the poor on Maundy Thursday. Those who, in pious observance of Christian ordinances, thus charged themselves with phosphorus were, let us hope, not aware that they were simply perpetuating the worship of Venus. Friday, again, is the *dies Veneris*, and fish, her own symbol, is therefore appropriate food for the day. The *poisson d'Avril* is the survival of the old Spring offering to Aphrodite, under whose auspices the constellation of the Fishes was then in ascendant influence ; and through the interrogatories of the old Confessional we can trace back some innocent, but significant, customs of the English country folk of to-day to the rites in honour of the goddess of Love, in the days when the world was young.

In connection with this pious fish-eating it is worth noting that their error as to the true character of the cetaceans betrayed our forefathers into breaking Lent, for under the impression that the whale, porpoise, and seal were fish, they ate them on fast-days. High prices, moreover, were paid for such meats, and "porpoise pudding" was a dish of state as late as the sixteenth century.

In other aspects also the fish was eminently a Christian symbol. It occurs frequently in the Roman catacombs, bearing on its back a bowl with wine and covered with wafers of bread ; and in many of the tombs are found small fish in wood or ivory, while the simple figure of a fish on a gravestone or monument was employed as an emblematic acrostic * to point out to his co-religionists the burial-place of a Christian without betraying the fact to their pagan persecutors. It has been imagined that the pointed oval

---

* I-ch-th-u-s being the initial letters of the Greek words for Jesus—Christ—of God—Son—Saviour.

so common not only for enclosing pictures, seals, mono-
grams, etc., but even for rings and ornaments, is the
symbol of the fish, and the representations of the Virgin
"in a canopy" or *vesica piscis*, are supposed therefore to
have a specially Christian significance ; but if it has any at
all, it is a very heathenish one.

CHAPTER IV.

Fashions in fish-eating—Pisces Regales—Fishes in Art—In Astronomy—Legends of the Zodiac—In Astrology—Fish-gems.

BUT eating is not, after all, solely a religious exercise, and
in the matter of fish, though the priests sometimes dictated
the bill of fare, the people as often chose their dishes for
themselves. Thus, in old Egypt, the priests abstained
from fish altogether, and therefore, when all the rest of
the people were obliged by their religion to eat a fried
fish before the door of their houses, they only burnt
theirs, without tasting them. So says Plutarch, and the
reason which he tells us the priests gave for their absten-
tion was, that fish was neither nice nor necessary. But
among the nation in general, the favourite kinds * were
the *bulti* (Labrus Niloticus), the *kishr* (Perca Nilotica),
the *benni* (Cyprius Benni or C. Lepidotus), the *shall*
(Silurus Shall), the *shilbeh* (the Silurus Schilbe Niloticus),
and *arabrab*, the *byad* (Silurus Bajad), the *karmoot* (Silurus
Carmuth).

As to the attitude of the Syrians towards such diet, I
find some difficulty. That their priests also abstained from
fish is tolerably certain, but it is difficult to reconcile the
statement, that in consequence of Derceto, a Syrian divinity,
having changed herself into a fish, the people of that

---

* According to Wilkinson.

country never touched any kind whatever ; and the other statement, that Queen Atergatis was so passionately fond of the food that she allowed none to be sold till the refusal of it had been offered to the royal kitchen. It is possible that the two traditions are really halves of a third, which states that Queen Gatis, who was also said to be inordinately addicted to fish-eating (tunny, conger, and carp, her favourites), was put to death by Mopsus the Lydian, who had her thrown into Lake Ascalon. That the princess should be deified and the fish of the lake abstained from, is strictly in sympathy with contemporary sentiment, and the conflicting testimony of the ancients I have quoted would thus be reconciled. But of course this is mere surmise.

That the Greeks ate fish, and had their fashions therein, is notorious, yet Homer never mentions fish in his banquets, and Ulysses is depicted as resorting to that diet only when in great extremity. In Rome, the fish mania, both as pets and as delicacies, was carried to such a pitch of insane, criminal extravagance, as to have been incredible, had not the savage satire and the fierce denunciation of contemporary literature assured us of the facts. It is enough to say that a single dish of fish might cost from £100 to £1000, and that pet eels were fed with human slaves. It is worth noting also that, in spite of the intolerable affectations of Roman connoisseurs as to the niceties of flavour between this fish, that had been caught on one side of a river, and that, which had been caught on the other, they all drenched their subtly-flavoured dishes with halec, garum, and other sauces, which were so strong and composite that it would have been hardly possible to distinguish a fresh fish from a putrid cat—except by the bones.

The ancient Britons were not, as a nation, fish-eaters, due

probably to the fact that our painted ancestors worshipped
the streams, and from this pagan reverence for the waters,
their naiad-folk, and the fishes they protected, I would
venture to surmise that the objection of the lower classes
at the present day to a fish diet has arisen.

Sea-fishing as an industry is said to have been intro-
duced into Albion by St. Wilfrid, and the Anglo-
Saxons, then abandoning paganism, came to indiscrimi-
nate fish-eating. In the fourteenth century sturgeon
was declared a royal fish, and statutes exist (of a later
date) restricting the consumption of porpoises, seals, and
"grampus," as meats too dainty for the million. That Henry
I. died of a surfeit of lampreys " is one of those things that
every schoolboy knows ; " but the extraordinary estimation
in which this fish was long held is a less familiar fact.
Royal edicts have been published regulating the price of
the dainty when the cupidity of fishmongers threatened
to send it up beyond the purses of the rich, and King John
sent special agents to the Continent to purchase lampreys.
Gloucester city used at one time to send every Christmas
a lamprey-pie to the sovereign.

Herring-pie also was once accounted a royal delicacy.
Yarmouth, by its charter, was pledged to furnish the king
annually with a hundred herrings baked in twenty-four
pasties, and more than one private estate on the coast was
held on a tenure of herring-pies. In Queen Elizabeth's
reign, sturgeon, "whales," and porpoises were among the
Pisces Regales, but it is not probable that her sister was an
enthusiast, inasmuch as her royal husband was of opinion
that fish was not proper food for human beings, "being
only congealed water." France had its notable ichthyo-
phagists in Louis XII., Francis I., Henry IV. (who kept
twenty-five royal fishmongers), and Louis XIV. In China

the sturgeon is a royal fish, and in the Sandwich Islands,* the bonito, albicore, and squid, are among the monopolies of the king's table. That any one should quarrel over the privilege of eating squids may seem strange to us who reject them except as bait, but they were esteemed by the ancients, notably the Greeks, and are at this day eaten by all the races on the Eastern seas, as well as the nations of Southern Europe and the Mediterranean † generally. Odious as the idea of eating an octopus may be, it is not, after all, so strange as the Japanese mania for the poisonous furuke, by eating which, in defiance of imperial edict, they are enabled to obtain, at one and the same time, the carnal pleasure of a tasty dish and the posthumous honours of the Happy Despatch.

As properly leading out from my note preceding on the Patron Saints of fishes, their place in legendary art may be here briefly referred to. Notable among the paintings in which fish, in connection with their patrons, are conspicuous, are Raphael's noble piece, the *Madonna della Pesce*, in which the child Tobias, with the fish in his hand, is being brought by St. Raphael to the Virgin ;

---

* There the "lords of the manor" have also the right to specify one kind of fish as exclusively for their own eating, whenever caught in their waters.

† "Along the western coast of France, and in the countries bordering on the Mediterranean and Adriatic, they form a portion of the habitual sustenance of the people, and are regularly exposed for sale in the markets, both in a fresh and dried condition. Salted cuttles and octopus are there eaten during Lent as commonly as salted cod are brought to table in England ; and, thus prepared, generally form a portion of the provisions supplied to the Greek fishing-boats and coasters. This strange diet is chiefly obtained from Tunis, and in the Levant and Greek markets its trade name is octopodia or polypi."— Prof. Martin Duncan (*Cassell's Nat. Hist.*).

and the other that represents Tobias hauling the fish
to land, with the Angel standing by. St. Peter in many
pictures of celebrity carries a fish, and in the pictures
of the " Calling of Peter and Andrew " and " Finding
the Tribute-Money," and the celebrated cartoon of " The
Miraculous Draught," his avocation is always conspicuously
represented. St. Zeno, bishop of Verona (said to have
been an enthusiastic angler), carries a fishing-rod in the
statue in the church at Verona, and in early pictures of the
Veronese school wears the habit of a bishop with a fish
hanging from the crook of his crozier. The picture by
Salvator Rosa of St. Anthony's fish-sermon is well known,
as is also the mosaic in St. Peter's, Rome, *Naviculo di
Giotto*, which represents St. Peter drawing his nets. The
same subject is engraved upon the Pope's ring, *l'anello
del piscatore*. An armed knight with his foot on a sea-
monster (a mediæval variation of the zodiacal Water-
carrier) may, or may not, be St. Andrew of Scotland ;
while in another artistic representation of the heavenly
system, in which the Apostles take the place of the pagan
signs of the zodiac and Saints are used instead of the
mythical figures of the constellations, I find St. Matthias
paired off against the Fishes.

In Astronomy the sea-things occupy their full share of
space, for among the principal constellations there are four
marine creatures as against seven quadrupeds and three
birds, and if we take the complete list the same proportion
is maintained. Their presence also in the zodiac gives us
one more link with the remotest past. Does not Proctor—
and with something more than mere surmise—read in the
configurations of the firmament the first suggestions of the
story of Noah's Flood ? and can we not by these recurrent

signs trace back—through the origin of Egyptian animal worship—through old Israel's twelve coincidences in the naming * of his sons—through the zodiac of Denderah, eight centuries before our era—to the very alphabet and rudiments of Aryan science ?

What antiquities, then, they are, these sea-myths of our stellar hemispheres ! Tumbling in open space, the happy Dolphin, belted with stars, the gift of grateful Olympus ; the luminous Sea-lizard ; Cetus, the shaggy whale, spangled from twinkling snout to twinkling tail, that, but for the strong bright-fronted Ram that intervenes, seems agape to swallow the suppliant Andromeda ; Hydra, dripping stars as it goes, and trailing its gem-lit convolutions across the hemispheres ; the Flying-fish,† feathered and beaked, darting its brief flight from the pole of the southern ecliptic ; the austral Fish, with radiant eyes uplifted to the grateful flood that the Waterer for ever pours upon it ; the Sword-fish, cleaving its bright way to encounter in the ocean of the firmament its hereditary foe ; the Tortoise, that in its starry concave holds the lyre whence Mercury first struck the music of the spheres.

Above all, The Fishes of the Zodiac—

> " The double Pisces, from their shining scale,
> Spread wat'ry influence and incline to sail "‡—

foster the sailor-spirit in men and teach navigators to be

---

* Zabulun, " that dwells at the haven of the sea," stands for the sign Pisces.

† So Pantagruel. " I saw here the sea-swallow, a fish as large as a dare-fish of Loire." In Chaldæan astronomy the northern of the Pisces is swallow-headed, as heralding the arrival of summer and its bird.

‡ This and succeeding quotations are from the translation of Manilius' poem by Creech.

boldly self-reliant, preside over sea-fights, and are the patrons of fishermen—whom they generously direct

> " To sweep smooth seas with nets, to drag the sand,
>   And draw the leaping captives to the land,
>   Lay cheating wires, or with unfaithful bait
>   The hook conceal, and get by the deceit."

But the children born under the sign are, by a poetical extension of the Venus tradition, hot-blooded, given to jealousies and strife :

> " But could I rule, could I the Fates design,
>   The rising Fishes ne'er should govern mine ;
>   They give a hateful, prattling, railing tongue,
>   Still full of venom, always in the wrong."

For the tradition is, that "when the skies grew weak and giants strove, and snaky Typhon shook the throne of Jove," Venus fled the tumultuous scene, and hiding herself in the Euphrates as a fish, inspired the scaly tribes with new passions, "and with the Ocean mixt her Fire." So, too, the Southern Fish claims Aphrodite's favour, for the legend says that it saved her daughter from drowning in the Lake Boethe ; and yet another claims for it that it is the progenitor of all the fishes in the firmament.

Next "glowing" Cancer,

> "As close in 's shell he lies, affords his aid
>   To greedy merchants and inclines to trade."

But over births his influence is hardly more auspicious than the Fishes', though in omen * it is happy—

> " The dream 's good,
>   The Crab is in conjunction with the Sun."

---

* Under the influence of a conjunction of Jupiter, Saturn, and Mars, which took place in the year 1604, Kepler was led to think that he had discovered means for determining the true year of our Saviour's birth. He made his calculations, and found that Jupiter and Saturn

And it is by the Gate of Cancer, Mercury standing at the starry portals, that souls descend to take possession of the bodies of men. Not that the reasons of the crustacean's exaltation commend it to popularity ; for when Hercules was fighting with the Hydra, Juno meanly sent Cancer to bite the hero's heel ; but Hercules merely stopped for a moment in his job, killed the crab, and then went on with the Hydra. The goddess, however, translated the smashed crustacean to the skies, the crabs thus rising

> " On stepping-stones
> Of their dead selves to higher things."

In astrology, fish forms were in great request, the mystery attaching to sea-things commending them to the special service of the necromancer. But besides the strange fish with which the man of dark science made his studio dreadful, and which in his computations played such high pranks as might have made Herschel weep, he professed a knowledge of occult influences in fishy products that opened up vast possibilities. Coral and amber, nacre and ambergris, were potentially dreadful. From the heads of fishes he took you the dread cimedia, that, properly handled, worked Darwinism backwards ; and from the tortoise the gem chelonia, which, smeared with honey and laid upon the tongue, bestowed the gift of divination, provided the stars were in auspicious conjunction. This precious thing bore the tortoise shape, and the Magi told wonderful stories of its powers in appeasing storms ; nevertheless the kind starred over with gold spots, if thrown together with a beetle into boiling

---

were in the constellation of the Fishes (a fish is the astrological symbol of Judæa) in the latter half of the year of Rome 747, and were joined by Mars in 748. . . Their first union in the East awoke the attention of the Magi, told them the expected time had come, and bade them set off without delay towards Judæa (the fish land).

water, would raise a tempest.* Once, therefore, find the
chelonia, and you were Moses and Prospero, or Cassandra
and the Witch of Endor, in one. Plutarch ('On Rivers')
says that the sangaris produces the gem called Ballen, "the
king," by the Phrygians. Ptolemy Hephaestion, the astro-
loger, describes a gem (asterites) found in the belly of a
huge fish named Pan, from its resemblance to that god.
This, if exposed to the sun, shot forth flames, and was a
powerful philtre. Helen used it for her own signet, engraved with a figure of the Pan fish, and owed to it all her
conquests. To these may be added the astrobolos, "the
fish-eye," and the "adularia," both of them gems of force in
the Black Art, and also, as being gifts of the sea, those
shells which, powdered into potions, made love-philtres.
And no wonder! What was the happy shell that held
Venus before she was vouchsafed to the earth? What
fortunate mollusc lent Amphitrite its pearly home for a
chariot? Yet supreme among all shells must ever remain
the rough rind that holds the pearl, the delight of poets,
the ambition of women, the favourite of all.

Pearls were supposed to be sea-dew, which the oyster
drank in, and by its own mystic chemistry transformed
into gems, and the differences in colour were fancifully
attributed to climatic influences. On cloudy nights the
oyster secreted dark pearls; and when the moon shone
brightly, "the perles were white, fair, and orient." They
were soft till the sun shone on them, and then they
hardened. One legend (it is a Moslem one) tells us that
devils dived for pearls for Solomon, but devils here means
only "jinns"; and it almost needed this interference of a
supernatural agency to account for man being the master
of such an exquisite possession.

* 'Gems and Precious Stones' (King).

CHAPTER V.

FISHES IN FABLE AND FAIRY-TALE.

Fishes in Fable—as a rule Foolish Folk—but the Crab wise—the Tortoise not always sagacious—nor the Flat-Fish—Fishes in Fairy-tale as a rule Benign—also in Folk-tale of all countries—Fishes the Patrons of distressed Heroes and Heroines — Tendency of Fishermen to become Princes—Grateful Fishes—The Jewel-finding Myth—Fish as Guardians of Treasure—Cities of the Plain now Lakes, and their inhabitants Fishes—Some Fish-mysteries.

IN the story of the "Cruel Crane Outwitted," the bird, finding the fish likely to die of drought in a fast-shrinking puddle, offers to carry them across to a large and pleasant lake of which he knows. After much suspicious demurring, the fishes go with the crane one by one, and are, of course, eaten up in succession. Left last of all, however, is an old crab, and the bird proposes to take it over too to join its old comrades. "Very good," says the crafty crustacean, "but as you cannot very well hold me in your beak as you did the fishes, suppose I hold you with my pincers." The crane agrees to this, and having arrived at the shambles, announces to the crab that he is now about to be eaten. "Not a bit of it," is the reply. "On the contrary, if you do not take me to the lake at once, I shall nip your head off your thin neck." So the crane, in great alarm, takes Cancer straight to the lake, but before getting off the bird's back the crab bites its head off.

This fable illustrates the difference of character in fables between the fish and the crustaceans. The former are

E

always used as the stupid persons of the incident—the
foolish folk who are found dancing in the nets just when
they should be most serious ; who get caught and beg the
fishermen to put them back, " so that we may grow larger
and better worth your eating ; " who catch hold of hooks in
order to pull the angler into the water ; who rush into the
net just to make fun of the fisherman, forgetting that, though
it is the same old net, with the same meshes that they used
to slip through when they were tiny fry, they have been
gradually getting bigger themselves ; who fall victims, in
fact, to every designing person who comes their way.

The crab, however, enjoys a character for sagacity, and
humour of a grim sort.   His " swike " with the crane was
excellent fooling ; and so again, when he kills the snake and
sees it lying stretched out along the ground, he addresses
the dead viper with the caustic moral—"This fate would
never have befallen you if you had lived as straight as you
have died."   The crab runs the fox a race, and as soon as
his opponent starts catches hold of its tail.   When the fox
reaches the winning-post it turns round to see how far the
crab has got, when the wily crustacean quietly drops off,
crosses the winning-line, and startles the fox with—"What !
come at last, are you ?   I've been here some time ! "

Tortoises also are occasionally credited with ingenuity.
Thus, when the great bird Kruth came to eat it, the tortoise
begged to have one chance of life given it, and therefore
offers to race the bird across the lake, Kruth to fly and
the tortoise to dive.   The bird agreeing, the testacean
calls its kindred together, and stations them, at short
distances apart, all round the lake, and having made
these preparations gives Kruth the signal to start—Off !
and down he dives under the water.   Away goes the
bird straight across the lake, but wherever he tries to
settle, up pops a tortoise, and Kruth, not knowing one

from another, concludes it is always the same old tortoise, and flies off in disgust. But this is exceptional, for
the tortoise as a rule is a fool. He begs eagles to take him
up into the sky, "to see the world," and gets dropped on to
rocks and eaten in return for his misplaced confidence.
He pretends he will tell the king of the birds a great secret
if he will carry him over a range of mountains, and is made
half-way to tell his secret, and then, as usual, dropped on
to the customary rock. So again when his good friends
the wild geese are carrying him to the Golden Cave on the
Himalaya Mountains, the people of a town over which they
pass, go into fits of laughter at seeing two geese with the
ends of a stick in their beaks and a tortoise hanging down
by his mouth from the middle. The tortoise cannot resist
the opportunity for a retort, but he has hardly got the first
word out of his mouth when down he comes smash on the
ground.

Flat-fish, again, have a distinctive character, their grotesque facial arrangements suggesting superciliousness, and
a general kind of wry-mouthed ill-nature. The fluke,
therefore, gets its mouth twisted round for sneering at the
coronation of the herring : in Grimm it is the sole, and
elsewhere the plaice ; while all the flat-fish are flattened
out for being disagreeable, the rays for stinging a god when
out fishing, and the turbot for upsetting a nymph it was
carrying, and so forth. But with these few exceptions the
fishes of fable are simply foolish folk.

In fairy-tale they are invariably benign. Thus in the
admirable Red Indian story of " Sheem, the Forsaken Boy."
the sturgeon that saves Owasso plays a beneficent part.
The wicked old magician, his father-in-law, takes him out
fishing, and just as Owasso is about to spear the sturgeon,
he makes his enchanted boat dart away from under the

striker's feet, and the young man falls into the water.
But the sturgeon magnanimously carries Owasso to the
shore (where it gets cooked and eaten for its pains), and
bye-and-bye the wicked Manito comes to well-merited grief
at his son-in-law's hands. Again, in the story of " The
Little Spirit, or Boy-man," the main incidents are fish ones.
The boy-man steals the fish of the giant brothers, and
incurs their dislike, and then upsets them by a stratagem
into a fishing-hole in the ice, and so kindles their dislike
into wrath. But he outwits them, and takes refuge inside
a fish which he calls to his assistance, but which he afterwards betrays and eats.

In Portuguese folk-tale the recurrence of the fish-figure
is very marked, and always in the same benign aspect. Thus
in the story of the Baker's Idle Son (that has its well-known
Russian and German counterparts), the fish that comes up
to him in the wood to eat his crumbs, and though caught
by the boy, is released when it begs for its life, continues
to befriend him till his fortunes are completed : the good
daughter of the wicked witch takes the form of an eel, to
assist the prince ; a whale, at the cost of its own life, rescues
the maiden from whose head the pearls used to fall when
she combed her hair ; in the Portuguese version of Cin-
derella—the Hearth-cat, as she is called—it is a fish which
plays the part of the good fairy or the white pigeons ;
St. Peter makes use of a fish to save his little god-
daughter from death ; a beautiful fish is caught, and sub-
mits to being sliced up into pieces, for the aggrandise-
ment and future welfare of the family of his captor. This
last story is one of many that are common to the nurseries
of the whole world. In the tale of the Gold Children,
the golden fish that is cut up into six pieces, to the great
good fortune of the fisherman and his family, is the same

as the beautiful fish of Breton fairy-lore, that makes its captor promise to eat its brains, as all manner of good luck will then overtake him ; and the same as the numerous other fishes who reward those who catch them with all the riches and pleasures of life. Common also to most fairy-lores are the flounder that was an enchanted prince, which gave to a fisherman all that his wife asked for, even to becoming Pope, but when she asked to be the Creator, the flounder, in indignation, sent her back to her original state ; the grateful fish in the story of Ferdinand the Faithful ; the accommodating fishes who, to help the drummer out of his difficulties, jumped out of the pond and arranged themselves in proper order on the grass ; the other fishes in Russian and Portuguese stories that assist heroes and heroines to accomplish impossible tasks ; the fish that so wonderfully refreshed the lovers when they were flying from the Dwarf's Island. In all these cases, and many more besides, the benign and philanthropic aspect of the fishes is consistently expressed, and even when these creatures are not actively employed in what may almost be called the routine of their amiabilities, they are found co-operating with men and women for their advantage in a most disinterested way. Fishermen are perpetually arriving at honours and wealth by the advice of the things they hook and net, and it is quite in the day's work if a fisher-lad becomes a prince and marries the king's daughter. When Biroquoi and his friends are arming the Prince, the fishes furnish the young warrior's "harness," as Don Quixote would call it. They gave him a brilliant cuirass of the scales of golden carps, and placed on his head the shell of a huge snail, which was overshadowed with the tail of a large cod, raised in the form of an aigrette ; a naiad girt him with an eel, from which depended a tremendous sword

made out of a long fish-bone ; and lastly, they gave him
the shell of a large tortoise for a shield. So that by the
time Babiole was equipped *cap-à-pie* there had been a considerable destruction of friendly fishes. When the seal-
fisher falls into the water, and is caught by the seals, what
do they do with him ? They take him down into Seal-
world, and there show him a harpoon of his and a wounded
seal, and they make him lay his hand on the wound which
he had inflicted, and swear that he will never hunt seals any
more. And then they take him, by a short cut, back to his
home again. Even when fishes swallow human beings,
they do so in the most friendly spirit imaginable. The
number of notable personages that have thus been amiably
gulped down, and afterwards restored to friends and sun-
light, is very large indeed, and the conduct of the fish is in
every case admirable. When, for instance, the "great fish"
swallowed Jonah, it did so with the best intentions, for, so
the Arabic legend says, it swam to shore, a three days'
journey, with its mouth above water all the way, for the
greater convenience of the prophet's breathing. The good
taste of such behaviour is undeniable.

But by far the most widely-spread legend of the sea-
things' philanthropy is that which makes them the guardians
of lost treasures, and the vehicle for their restoration to
their proper owners — the fish-with-the-ring-inside-it myth,
that every country in turn has adapted from the original
story that was told on the banks of the Oxus to Aryan
children, long before Britain, as we know it, had come to
the surface of the sea.

The salmon with a ring in its mouth, that figures in the
arms of Glasgow, is one of the many fishes credited with
being the means of lost jewels returning to their owners.
A certain queen gave a soldier, with whom she had fallen

in love, a ring that had been presented to her by her con-
sort ; but the king discovered the intrigue, and having
obtained the ring, threw it into the Clyde, and then de-
manded it of his disloyal lady.   In her alarm she sought
help from the holy Kentigern, and the saint, proceed-
ing to the river, forthwith caught a salmon which, on being
opened, was found to have swallowed the all-important
jewel.   So the queen regained the good graces of the king,
and, it is satisfactory to be able to add, lived a better life
ever afterwards.*   A Tyne salmon caught in its mouth as
it fell, and was the means of restoring to its owner, a ring
that had dropped off a bridge at Newcastle ; and a Thames
pike has been known to be equally opportune and useful.
The best known of all such narratives is, of course, that of
Polycrates' signet-ring, which was thrown into the sea and
recovered from the body of a fish presented to the king by
a fisherman.   But this is by no means the original of the
episode, for Solomon recovered his throne by a fish restoring him the talisman ring by virtue of which he held
dominion over all the devils ; † and more ancient still is the

---

* A variation is to be found in the following :— " The legend of
the fish and the ring," says the Rev. Dr. Dibdin in his ' Northern
Tour,' " is extant in well-nigh every class-book in Scotland ; old Spots-
wood is among the earliest historians who garnished the dish from the
Latin monastic legends, and Messrs. Smith, M'Lellan, and Cleland
have not failed to quote his words.   They report of St. Kentigern, that
a lady of good place in the country having lost her ring as she crossed
the river Clyde, and her husband waxing jealous, as if she had bestowed the same on one of her lovers, she did mean herself unto
Kentigern, entreating his help for the safety of her honour, and that he
going to the river after he had used his devotion, willed one who was
making to fish to bring the first that he caught, which was done.   In
the mouth of the fish he found the ring, and sending it to the lady, she
was thereby freed of her husband's suspicion."

† Sale gives the following version :—" Solomon entrusted his signet
with one of his concubines, which the devil obtained from her and

recovery of Sakuntala's ring by a fish, which thus enabled King Dasyanta to marry the lady of his love.

From this fancy of the Aryan poet has descended an immense progeny of treasure-retrieving fishes, and the ring of Sakuntala, like the magic circlet of the Persian story, has begotten innumerable rings exactly like itself.

In the 'Arabian Nights' is the well-known tale of the priceless diamond which the fisherman takes from a fish, and which, placed on a shelf in the cottage, gives so much light that they are saved all expenditure in oil, and which when sold makes the family rich for ever and for ever. In Scandinavian myths is that of the long-lost crown, which the fishes kept safely down among the rocks, till the real heir to the throne came a-fishing, when they rolled it into his net; in Russian, that of Ivan, who finds the all-important ring by the help of the perch—the herrings try to lift the casket to the surface, but fail, and so two dolphins come and put their shoulders to the wheel, and the ring is regained; in the Portuguese is one that tells us how St. Peter's god-daughter is ordered by a malicious queen to dive into the sea to bring up a ring which she has purposely thrown into the waves, but St. Peter restores it to the little girl by making a fish swallow it and be caught for the King's table. In the other story of the Basket of almonds, the king of the fishes himself brings up the key which the monarch has thrown into the sea, its recovery being the price of the hero's marrying the princess; in the (?) Italian story of the White Snake the

---

sate on the throne in Solomon's shape. After forty days the devil departed and threw the ring into the sea. The signet was swallowed by a fish, which, being caught and given to Solomon, the ring was found in its belly, and thus he recovered his kingdom."

three grateful fish bring to the servant, in a mussel-shell, the ring that brings every one joy ; in the Russian the crayfish recovers the merchant's magic snuff-box. Nor are these, probably, a half of the fairy legends that have all grown out of Kalidasa's beautiful creation.

Specially noteworthy among these jewel-restoring, and so (by a not unreasonable extension) treasure-defending, fishes is the pike. It is, says Afanassieff, a fish of great repute in northern mythology. One of the old Russian songs, still sung at Christmas, tells how the pike comes from Novogorod, its scales of silver and gold, its back woven with pearls, and costly diamonds gleaming in its head instead of eyes. And this song is one which promises wealth, a fact connecting the Russian fish with that Scandinavian pike which was a shape assumed by Andvarri, the dwarf-guardian of the famous treasure, from which sprang the woes recounted in the Volsunga Saga and the Nibelungenlied. According to a Lithuanian tradition there is a certain lake which is ruled by the monstrous pike Strukis. It sleeps only once a year, and then only for a single hour. It used always to sleep on St. John's night, but a fisherman once took advantage of its slumber to catch a quantity of its scaly subjects. Strukis awoke in time to upset the fisherman's boat, but fearing a repetition of the attempt, it now changes every year the hour of its annual sleep.*

Apart from any special characteristic in the nature of their service to man, fish play in the folk-tale a most important part. In every country the cultus of the water-spirit has more or less obtained, and the aqueous feature of local myth being thus popularly accepted, the prominence of water-things is a natural result, just as among tribes to

* Ralston's 'Russian Folk-tales,' chapter iv.

whom the sea, as a means of livelihood, is as important as the land—whether we go to Polynesia or Scandinavia to find them—we find marine and fishery folk-lore predominant. Thus the old goblin from Norway, who came a-wooing to the Elfin-hill, and spoke so pleasantly about the stately Norwegian rocks and the waterfalls, and the salmon that leaped in the spray while the water-god played to them on a golden harp, could never tell a story without something about a fish in it. And again, when he spoke of the cheery winter nights within doors, he described particularly how the salmon would gambol in the water outside his cave, and dash themselves against the rocks, but could not come in.

But into this prodigious literature of fairy-tale fish, in which the finny ones merely play the part of wonder-workers, or represent the victims of sorcery, I have no space, though all the will, to plunge. But how can I close this chapter without referring to that little fish of the Arabian Nights which was really a pomegranate seed, which the cock (who was really a princess) overlooked with such disastrous consequences to all concerned? Or to those other fishes, white, red, blue, and yellow, that the fisherman found swimming in the enchanted lake between the four small hills, and which when brought into the Sultan's palace led to such notable results?

This formation of a lake as a punishment for the wickedness of the People of the Plain is a widely-spread tradition.* Thus, so local legends say, Lake Tanganika was called into existence. "Years and years ago, where you see this great lake," so runs the African story, "was a wide plain, inhabited by many tribes and nations, who owned

* The mythologist may read in the following story a significance which supports Gubernatis.

large herds of cattle and flocks of goats, just as you see
Uhha to-day. On this plain there was a very large
town, and in it lived a man and his wife, who possessed a
deep well which contained countless fish, that furnished
both the man and his wife with an abundant supply for
their wants; but as their possession of these treasures
depended upon the secrecy which they preserved respect-
ing them, no one outside their family circle knew anything
of them. A tradition was handed down for ages through
the family, from father to son, that on the day they showed
the well to strangers they would be ruined and destroyed.
It happened, however, that the wife, unknown to her husband, loved another man in the town, and bye-and-bye, her
passion increasing, she conveyed to him by stealth some of
the delicious fish from the wonderful well, and afterwards,
when her husband had gone, she took him to the enclosure
and showed him what appeared a circular pool of deep
clear water, which bubbled upwards from the depths, and
she said, ' Behold! this is our wondrous fountain ; is it not
beautiful ? And in this fountain are the fish.' The man
had never seen such things in his life, for there were no
rivers in the neighbourhood, except that which was made by
this fountain. His delight was very great, and he sat for
some time watching the fish, and bye-and-bye one of the
boldest of the fish came near where he was sitting, and he
suddenly put forth his hand to catch it. But that was the
end of all !—for the Muzimu, the spirit, was angry. And the
world cracked asunder, the plain sank lower and lower and
lower—the bottom cannot now be reached by our longest
lines—and the fountain overflowed and filled the great gap
that was made by the earthquake, and now what do you
see ? The Tanganika ! All the people of that great plain
perished, and all the houses and fields and gardens, the

herds of cattle and flocks of goats and sheep, were swallowed in the waters."

But why can we not find some friendly fish, in all this host of friendly fishes, to clear up some of our water mysteries ? What, for instance, is the meaning of this story from the Arabic :—"A traveller near the Caspian Sea saw some fishermen catch a large fish and perforate its ears, when suddenly a ruddy-coloured maiden, of a beautiful countenance, with long hair, came out of one ear, began to smite her cheeks and to tear her hair. God, the Creator, had provided her with a short white apron, which extended from her waist to her knees." And what fish was it that gave its shell, six fathoms long and three in breadth, to make a bridge across the palace-moat of the King of the Genii ; and what was the monster, "resembling a green meadow," on which Sindbad and his fellow-voyagers landed to cook their meals, and to which we are indebted for all Sindbad's subsequent adventures? What were the fish that ate the bitumen that flowed from the Inaccessible Mountain and returned it to the waves as ambergris, or the others that so pleased the fair Persian when the Caliph played at being Fisherman ? What was the sea-beast St. Margaret overcame, or that other with which Beorwulf fought for a night and a day ? Can any one tell me the species of Thiodvitnir's fish that plunges everlastingly in the roaring Thund ?

CHAPTER VI.

FISH IN HERALDRY.*

Frequency of Fish-crests—Derived from Names or Puns upon Names —from Privileges of Fishery—from Incidents of Family History —Towns with Fishing Rights—Badges of the Piscatorial Franchise—Perpetuation of Old-world Myths — Fishes of Fancy— Mermaids and their Relatives — Crustaceans—Shell-fish and Shells—Fish-bones as a Crest—Fish on Signboards.

HERALDRY has been called "the science of fools with long memories," but, regarded more sympathetically, the title which heralds claim for it, that it is "the shorthand of history," is better deserved. It is an epitome, also, of the strangest fictions and the most beautiful fancies of past times. For though heraldry proper does not date beyond the twelfth century, its subject reaches back through all the world's traditions and myths to the very remotest antiquity.

Sylvanus Magnus, in his anxiety to prove that Adam was a gentleman, has given him a coat of arms. But heraldry needs no such absurdity of patronage to commend it. For though as a science it may be modern enough, it has been a loadstone both to myths and historical facts,

* The heraldry of fish is a curious study, and in the works of Moule and Mrs. Bury Palliser is invested with a remarkable interest from the intelligence with which history, folk-lore, legends, and superstitions, are used to illustrate the various devices and to throw light upon both badges and mottoes. In the charming pages of Planché the facts of heraldry, and the broad rules upon which that fantastic science works, are set forth with a delightful amplitude of queer lore.

and in its lucid preservation of them has been veritable
amber.

In badge and device, shield and crest, the fish-form is
very frequently recurrent, and research into the figure-
heads of the vessels of antiquity would probably, while
extending the legitimate area of heraldry, show that the
fish and sea-monsters which are so conspicuous in modern
coats-of-arms are, in some cases, the survival of the badges
with which the sea-going heroes of old delighted to adorn
their war craft. That heralds have not taken any notice of
this, the earliest European mode of expressing upon property the distinctive emblem of the owner, is somewhat
remarkable, for in this old-world fashion a clue might
perhaps be picked up that would connect the dolphins,
salmons, pike, and so forth of the present day, with the
primitive clan-animals and totems to which I have already
alluded.

Meanwhile, there is an abundance of fish-heraldry connected with those popular beliefs which form the subjects
of my previous chapters ; and, indeed, the relation which
the present chapter bears to the rest of this pamphlet is an
apt simile of the relation of heraldry in general to all
previous history. For it traverses every subject, and concerns itself with each phase of animism in turn. I shall
treat this chapter, therefore, as an epitome of those that
precede it, and follow fish heraldry in particular through
the same aspects, and in the same sequence, as I have
dealt with fish-lore in general.

Fish crests and badges have, it seems to me, been
acquired by three means—from the resemblance of name,
from privileges of fishery, and from incidents in personal
history. To the first class belong the impresas of the
families of Barbel, Breame, Chub, Codd, Crabbe, Dolphin,

Eales, Fish, Fry, Goujon, Haddock, Hake, Herring, Karp-
fen, Loach, Mackerel, Mullet, Pike, Roach, Seal, Shelley,
Smelt, Sprat, Sturgeon, Tench, Troutbeck, Whalley, Whiting,
and no doubt many others. A number more take their
cognisance from local names, such as Butt (flounder),
Chabot (miller's thumb), Dare (dace), Geddes and Lucy
(pike), Sparling (smelt), Tubbe (gurnard), Gobyon (gudgeon),
Cobbe (herring-fry), Garvine (garvie or sprat), and Carter
(carter-fish or sole) ; while very many others adopt as a
crest either some fish which bears a name of proximate
resemblance, as Bar (barbel), Sammes (salmon), Conghurst
(congers), Piketon (pike), Garling (gar-fish), Heringot
(herring), Tarbutt (turbot), Ellis or Elwis (eels) ; or else
one upon which, *more heraldico*, they can pun or make a
joke, as the head of a bull for the Gurneys (a gurnard
being also called the "bull's head") ; a fish-skeleton for
armorial bearings because an otter was the crest. The
Caters have a salmon because that fish was often the
" standard " of an entertainment that had been properly
catered for ; the Cheneys a burbot, or coney-fish, with a
rabbit ; the Dishingtons a scallop-shell, the pilgrim's dish.
The Lucy family has the pike's head, which is arrived at
in two ways: first as the head of the luce (the pike), and
second as the fleur-de-luce (the *fleur-de-lis*), which in its
shape is like the head of a halberd or pike.

Another variety of the fish-crest (but still connected with
the name) is that in which any fish for which a particular
river happens to be famous, is adopted in the arms of
families who take their name from that river or an estate
upon it. For instance, Yarrell bears the ruffe which
abounds in the Yare ; Way (from Wey), a salmon ; Streat-
ley, an eel-spear, that place being noted for that form of ·
sport. The Broughams bear a pike, from the abundance

of that fish in the Lowther; and the Glynns a salmon-spear, from the fishery at Glynn-Ford, on the Fowey.

As other instances of "privilege" (personal) may be noted the Lostwithiel crest of fish, the Earls of Cornwall having feudal rights of fishery in the Fowey, and the horn of tenure of the Hungerford burgesses; while among other English crests typical of the franchise of rivers are eel-baskets, oyster-dredges, fish-weirs, nets, and fish-hooks. The cognizance of the "Stern Falconbridge"—"the thrice victorious Lord of Falconbridge, Knight of the noble Order of St. George, Worthy Saint Michael, and the Golden Fleece, great Mareschal to Henry VI., of all the wars within the realm of France"*—was "the fysshe hoke." In Germany, this heraldic indication of rights in waters is very frequent, the fishing-spear, or "pheon,"† recurring abundantly in family escutcheons.

Analogous to this, of course, is the representation on the civic seals of fishing towns, of the particular fish that was most important. Thus Kingston-on-Thames bears the salmon, in reference to "the privilege of fishery" long enjoyed by the town. "By charter of Philip and Mary, a fishing-weir is held by the Corporation of Kingston in consideration of repairing the bridge, which was formerly of wood, but has been lately rebuilt with stone, and the emblems of their privilege, three salmon, are sculptured over the centre arch." For the same reason the burghs of Peebles, Lanark, and Helmsdale, show the same fish on their seals — the salmon fishery at Helmsdale (in Sutherlandshire) being one of the ancient privileges of

---

* The fishing-spear, or "pheon," better known now as the broad-arrow, has been the royal mark of possession from the days of Cœur-de-Lion.

† ' Henry VI.,' Part I., act iv., scene 7.

the dukedom. The town seal of Coleraine shows the
salmon ; and the Lords of the Isles, as masters of many
fisheries, bear the same fish. The town of Stafford (Izaak
Walton's birthplace) is on the Sow, a river noted for its
trout and grayling. A charter from King John confirmed
the privileges which had been held by the town from
remote antiquity, and the corporation seal, showing the
fish in the stream, with the castle on the bank, alludes to
this right of fishing. So, too, Newcastle (on Trent) bears
an allusion to a "franchise" of fishery. Yarmouth has, of
course, herrings, and has carried them ever since King
John gave the burgesses their charter with the right of
the fishery, of which till then the privilege had vested in
the Barons of the Cinque Ports. Wexford displays the
hake ; and on the seal of Congleton (in Cheshire) two
congers glare at each other. Kilrenny, in Fifeshire, carries
fish-hooks on its shield as typical of its chief source of
revenue. Dunwich, Southwold, and Inveraray, all confess
their gratitude to the herring ; and Truro, Looe, Fowey, and
other Cornish towns, to the pilchard.

As illustrative of the third class, the fish-crests com-
memorative of incidents of personal history are the Constantinople dolphins of the Courteneys ; the whale of the
Enderbys, whose ancestors were mighty fishers in the
Northern Seas ; the barbels of the Colstons, one of those
fishes having the credit of stopping a leak in a ship in
which a Colston was embarked ; the shark of the Watsons,
Sir Brook Watson having lost his leg from the bite of a
shark in the harbour of Havannah.

For the connection of heraldry with the sea-myths of
antiquity it would really be only necessary to instance the
dolphin. It is with heralds the "chief of fish"; and just
as in Hellenic devices it was always used to represent the

F

fish-world in general, being placed at the feet of Venus, on the tripod of Apollo, in the beard of Poseidon, at the heels of Orpheus, and employed perpetually to symbolize the ocean itself,—so in the modern art of emblematic designing it is the hieroglyph of fish in general. Thus a great many towns that owe their prosperity to their fisheries bear a dolphin as their cognizance. Two dolphins embowed within a shield are upon the seal of Brighton. Poole carries a dolphin and mermaid. So, too, among many others on the Continent, Dunkirk, Dornheim, Otranto, Bernbach, Onoltzbach, Swartzac, bear the dolphin as a "fish."

Old gems show us Neptune on a dolphin, Arion on another, Amphitrite in her shell drawn by a team of dolphins, and ships always attended by friendly dolphins. Emperors of Rome had the dolphin and anchor* for the device of their seals, and under the Greek empire the dolphin continued an imperial cognizance. So in later times English admirals took the sea-god or the dolphin for their supporters. Italian academies bore the emblem of Arion with his harp—

> "A fiddler on a fish through waves advanced ;
> He twanged his catgut, and the dolphin danced."

Princesses borrowed Amphitrite's shell and steeds, and European kings adopted the ensigns of bygone empires. Fortune on a dolphin was the device of Charles, Archduke of Austria. Admiral Chabot had the dolphin and anchor of Titus and Vespasian, as also had that Adolphus of Nassau who was killed at the Battle of the Spurs. Charles V.

---

* A dolphin twisted round the anchor, with the legend "Hasten slowly " (so the English family of On-slow). Analogous devices are the crab and butterfly of Augustus, and the tortoise rigged with sails of the Tuscan Dukes.

used the dolphins for supporters, as bettering in swiftness the azure greyhounds which formerly held that place of honourable trust ; and Portugal among its royal crests has the dolphin and ship. Another fish-antiquity that has survived is the remora. Thus Giovanni Battista Bottigella, of Padua, who fought in the Italian wars under Ferranti Gonzaga, took for device a ship in full sail, with the remora, or sucking-fish, attached to it, and the motto, *sic frustra.* Another motto for a similar crest is *Sic parvis magna cedunt,* and it is in this sense that Spenser employs the figure in his verse. The mythical fragrance of the cuttle-fish suggested to Domenichi to give the Cardinal Ferrara as device a sepia, with the motto, *Sic tua non virtus,* " meaning that as the cuttle-fish by its sweet odour attracts other fish around it, so the Cardinal, by the sweetness and affability of his disposition, drew all men after him." By the ancients, again, the seal was supposed to enjoy immunity from lightning, and among those who borrowed the protection of its skin was the Emperor Augustus, who always wore a belt of seal-fur. The idea arose from the fancy that the seal sleeps most profoundly during thunderstorms, and a seal slumbering peacefully on a rock in the midst of a stormy sea, still survives as one of the devices of the Dukes of Mantua. The crab again was believed by the ancients to grow only during the waxing of the moon ;* hence the crab of the Costi family, looking gratefully at the moon which warms the sea and makes the shelled thing comfortable, with the motto, " I take my form from its varied aspect."

From the old fiction of the sea-mouse piloting the

---

† " That planet," says Pliny, " is comfortable in the night-time, and with her warm light mitigateth the cold of the night.'

whale,* James V. of Scotland took his device of the whale and little fish, with the motto " Urget majora."

As perpetuating other old superstitions, should be cited the sea-lions borne by the Earls of Thanet (where, says Moule, " the inhabitants, partaking of the amphibious character of the sea-lion, live by sea and land, making the most of both elements as farmers and fishermen ") ; the black sea-lions of the Harlands ; the blue one of the Duckworths. The sea-horses, as an emblem of naval dominion, are among the insignia of our Admiralty ; and, among other coats-of-arms, are to be found in that of David Garrick. The Earls of Cardigan also display the sea-horse.

Heraldic variations of other terrestrial monsters of fancy are the sea-griffin (to be seen on a pillar in Iffley Church), the sea-unicorn of the Prussian arms, and the antlered fish.

The mermaid and her relatives are especially popular as devices ; and the half-human half-fish monster that from the Oannes of ancient Chaldæa to the Nibanaba of the Canadian Indian, has always held a place in popular belief, is a very conspicuous, and indeed beautiful, device in heraldry. In French heraldry the mermaid is called the Siren ; in Germany she has two tails ; in the Italian she carries a harp ; and in many cases in each country she is crowned. In England it is a very ancient crest ; and among others the Lords Byron, the Earls of Portsmouth (a black mermaid with golden hair), with the families of Bonham, Broadhurst, Garnyss, Hastings, Johnson, Lapp, Lauzun, Mason, Rutherford, Moore, and many

---

* " For whereas the whale hath no use of his eies (by reason of the heavie weight of his eie-brows that cover them), the other swimmeth before him.'"

others, display the sea-maiden in their armorial bearings. With her comb and looking-glass she smiles at us
from the shields of the Holmes, Ellises, Lapps ; and as a
supporter holds up the arms of the Viscounts Boyne and
Hood, the Earls of Howth and Caledon, and is borne by
the heads of the families of Sinclair of Rosslyn, and Scott
of Harden. Two mermaids crowned are the supporters
of the Boston arms. La Mellusine, "a very beautiful
syren in a bath, who with one hand combs her thick hair
over her shoulders, and with the other holds a mirror," is
an instance of its very frequent device in French heraldry ;
and another, on a coronet, holding a bottle and a glass,
a specimen of the Belgian "Mermaid."

Her kindred, the tritons, are also familiar badges. As
a crest, a triton leaving the sedges is borne by the Tatton
Sykes ; a merman with a hawk's bill is the crest of the
Lany and Cratfield families. Two Tritons support the
Lyttelton arms, and other instances are displayed on
the shields of the Earls of Sandwich, and some of the
Campbells.

Of fishes, religious and ecclesiastical, the science takes
comprehensive notice, and from the walls of Denderch and
the tombs of the martyrs, the fish symbol has come down
to our own day, and the Pisces may be seen on the doorway
of Iffley Church, in the nave of Peterchurch in Hereford-
shire, and elsewhere. Whales are the insignia of Whalley
Abbey ; bream of Peterborough ; haddock of Petershausen ;
herring of St. Edmund's, and also of the Black Friars
Priory at Yarmouth. The arms assumed by monasteries
were sometimes those of their benefactors, as the pike of
Calder Abbey, largely endowed by the Lucy family, and
the salmon of St. Augustine's at Bristol, in memory of the
fishery attached to that abbey by the Lords of Berkeley.

Many prelates and some primates have borne fish crests.
Thus Peter Courtenay, Bishop of Exeter, and afterwards of
Rochester, bears the dolphin of Constantinople—a previous
Peter of the house having attained to the purple, and
transmitted it to his sons Robert and Baldwin. An azure
dolphin curves itself upon the arms of John Fyshar,
another Bishop of Rochester, who also bore three eel-spears
—Rochester Cathedral being dedicated to St. Andrew,
who was put to death with those instruments. William
James, Bishop of Durham, also bore a black dolphin ;
Henry Robinson, Bishop of Carlyle, a flying-fish ; John
Cameron, Bishop, and James Beaton, Archbishop, of Glasgow, carry the salmon of the city arms ; Cardinal Benli-
venga, a grayling ; Richard Cheney, Bishop of Gloucester,
the ling ; Cardinal Enrique de Guzman, two pots of eels ;
William Attwater, Bishop of Lincoln, three crayfish ; and
so on through a lengthy catalogue of prelates who have
gone to the fish-world for their crests. Archbishop Herring,
and Thomas Sprat, Bishop of Rochester, display on their
coats the fishes of their own name.

Of the higher dignities of fish in heraldry, imperial and
royal examples have already been given. Among the
remainder, barbel appear in the royal arms of Bohemia
and Hungary, and again in the arms of Queen Margaret
of Anjou ; salmon on those of the Princes of Lorraine ;
a dried cod crowned is the arms of Iceland,[*] and borne
by the Kings of Denmark ; the crab, "an emblem of incon-
stancy," says Moule, appears on the shield of Francis I.,
and, according to Sir Samuel Meyrick, is an allusion to
the advancing and retrograde movements of the English
army at Boulogne.

Crustaceans, indeed, are curiously frequent. "The lob-

---

[*] " Of Iceland to write is little nede, save of stock-fish " (Hakluyt).

ster, as an enemy to serpents, was," says Moule, "sometimes used as an emblem of temperance, and two lobsters
fighting as an emblem of sedition." The union of a
lobster with the human form is an impresa of very old
date, but the families on the Continent that bear this
crustacean for a badge probably refer it back to no earlier
times than the chivalric days when knights went forth to
fight in that armour of overlapping plates which were
called "ecrivisses." Prawns and shrimps are among the
heraldic bearings of the Crafords and Atseas of Kent;
and the crayfish, also an English crest, was the badge
of the Prince of Orange, and betrayed that warrior to
imprisonment when he had hoped to escape identifi-
cation among a heap of the killed after the battle of
St. Aubin du Cormier. The crab frequently recurs—the
golden crabs of the Scropes, Danbys, and Bythesees being
instances. The turtle is not common, there being perhaps
only six in English heraldry; and among the miscellanea of
the sea are found the starfish, sea-urchins (Echinidæ), and
numerous shellfish.

A scallop on a shield shows, or should show, that an
ancestor had been in the Crusades, as it was the cognizance
of St. James, and after him of all who fought against the
infidels, and so of all pious pilgrims. The badge of the
Order of St. James of Spain is a sword with a cross
handle and a scallop on the pommel. The same shell
forms the badge and collar of the Order of St. James
in Holland, and Saint Louis instituted the "Order of the
Ship and Escallop" for the decoration of the nobility who
accompanied him to the Holy Land. The collar of the
Order of St. Michael, founded by Louis XI., was garnished
with golden scallops. The cockle, whelk, and several of
the genera Turbo and Cyprœa found among modern crests

and shields, date back to the palmy days of Phœnicia,
when Tyre and other cities of the Mediterranean stamped
their medals and coins with them.   The nautilus, a favourite
emblem in Southern Europe, bears in the badge of the
Affidati Academy the motto, " Safe above and below," in
allusion to the old-world description of its habits.

" But among the greatest wonders of nature is that fish which of
some is called nautilos, of others pompilos.   This fish, for to come
aloft above the water turneth upon his backe, and raiseth or heaveth
himselfe up by little and little ; and to the end he might swim with
more ease as disburdened of a sinke, he dischargeth all the water
within him at a pipe.   After this, turning up his two foremost clawes, or
armes, hee displaicth and stretcheth out betweene them a membrane
or skin of a wonderful thinnesse ; this serveth him instead of a saile in
the aire above water.   With the rest of his armes or clawes he roweth
and laboureth under water, and with his taile in the mids, he directeth
his course, and steereth as it were with an helme.   Thus holdeth he
on, and maketh way in the sea, with a faire shew of a foist or galley
under saile.   Now if he be afraid of anything in the way, hee makes
no more adoe but draweth in water to baillise his bodie, and so
plungeth himselfe downe, and sinketh to the bottom."

But, of course, the most celebrated and popular of shell
crests and devices was the pearl-oyster.   Charged with
its precious freight, it appears in a hundred forms, the
legend always repeating one or other of the curious and
beautiful fancies of antiquity.   Every royal Margaret, by
right of name, claimed the precious thing as her emblem ;
princes and nobles bore it on their impresas, and the
coronets of nobility take the degrees of rank from the
pearls upon them.

In German heraldry, fish as devices are even more
common, and their positions on the shields are infinitely
more varied than in the armorial bearings of England.
In France, also, where heraldry is more generally popular
than in Britain, there is a striking fertility in design, and

the fish form is very frequent. Among the curiosities of foreign heraldry must certainly be accounted the fish skeletons which we find as baronial crests on the Continent. That Amsterdam is built on herring bones is an old saying ; but why Bavaria, Franconia, and Switzerland should adopt such a singular, such a beggarly, badge, is a phenomenon still requiring explanation.

On signboards the fish is a figure of common recurrence. The trout is a favourite angler's cognizance, and "the golden perch," the gudgeon, the salmon, and the pike are among the individual fishes that swing before the doors of riverside inns. The Elephant and Fish—unless fish means "dragon," which in tradition is the hereditary foe of the elephant—is a device that puzzles the herald ; nor is the Cock and Dolphin more obvious in its significance. The dolphin, of course, is everywhere, in all kinds of curious combinations, and passing through as large a range of colours as the fabled creature when dying.

Moule only glances at piscine heraldry in his admirable work. "Frequently," he says, "the sign of the fish is seen without any further specification ; in this case it is probably meant for the dolphin, which is the signboard fish *par excellence.* The fish sign is a very common public-house decoration at the present day, probably for the same reason as the swan, because he is fond of liquor—nay, to such an extent goes his reputation for intemperance, that to 'drink like a fish' is a quality of no small excellence with publicans." In Carlisle, however, there are two signs of the Fish and Dolphin, a rather puzzling combination, unless it has reference to the dolphin's chase after the shoal of small fishes. The Fish and Bell, Soho, may either allude to a well-known anecdote of a certain numskull, who, when he caught a fish which he desired to keep for

dinner on some future occasion, put it back into the river
with a bell round its neck, so that he should be able to
know its whereabouts the moment he wanted it ; or it may
be the usual bell added in honour of the bell-ringers. A
quaint variety of this sign is the Bell and Mackerel, in the
Mile End Road. The Three Fishes was a favourite device
in the Middle Ages, crossing or interpenetrating each
other in such a manner that the head of one fish was at the
tail of another.

" The Three Herrings, the sign of James Moxton, a book-
seller in the Strand, near York House, in 1675, is evidently
but another name for the Three Fishes ; at the present
day it is the sign of an ale-house in Bell Yard, Temple
Bar. Several taverns with this sign are mentioned in the
French tales and plays of the seventeenth century. Two
of them seem to have been very celebrated, one in the
Faubourg St. Marceau, the other near the Palais de Justice.
This last one seems to have been particularly famous, for
it is named as a rival to the celebrated Pomme de Pin.
The Fish and Quart, at Leicester, must be passed by in
silence, as the combination cannot immediately be accounted for. Were it in France a solution would be easier,
for in French slang a 'poisson,' or fish, means a small
measure of wine. The Fish and Eels at Roydon, in Essex,
the Fish and Kettle, Southampton, and the White Bait,
Bristol, all tell their own tale, and need no comment. The
Salmon is seen occasionally near places where it is caught.
The Salmon and Ball is the well-known ball of the silk-
mercers in former times added to the sign of the salmon ;
whilst the Salmon and Compasses is the masonic emblem
that is added to the sign. Both these occur in more than
one instance in London."

CHAPTER VII.

FISHES IN MODERN FOLK-LORE.

Survival of Zoolatry in Modern Folk-lore—Mermaid Superstitions—
Water-horses and Water-bulls—How Fishes got their Shapes—
Feminine influences Sinister—Parsons of ill-omen to Fishermen
—Fish annoyed by Bells—Fish-prognostications—As Weather-
prophets—Fishes in Medicine—Superstitions as to Origin of
certain Fishes.

FACE to face with the living myths and superstitions of
the present, one feels, as I think it is Max Müller says,
like a geologist who in a country ramble should suddenly find himself confronted with a herd of megatheria.
For the world has not all grown old together, and there
are still in existence to-day people who have not aged
a bit in their intelligence since the "once-upon-a-time"
period which we—the precocious youngsters and the wise-
acres of the human family—only now retain as the com-
mencement of children's fairy-tales. We ourselves, for
instance, have long ago learned to look down as from
a superior pedestal upon the beast-world, and loftily
bespeak sympathy for the "poor dumb brute." But it is
not so all the world over; for there are nations breathing
the same air with us, sharing the same sun and moon,
launching boats on the same seas, who still to-day, in
the nineteenth century, in the age of electricity, speak
respectfully of beasts, birds, and fishes as of equals.
There are actually some also who still look up to and

reverence the things in fur, feathers, and scales as their
superiors.

The Red Indian calls them his "younger brothers," and
though compelled to eat them, he does so with apologies.
He excuses himself for the painful necessity of making a
meal off his "dear cousin"; deprecates the anger of the
eaten thing's relations by formulas of propitiation, and
hopes by posthumous ceremonials of respect to the skull
and bones and skin, to condone the consumption of the
meat and fat.   This is all, no doubt, grotesque enough,
but it is very much like meeting a megatherium in a
country lane.   One begins to feel the clothes slipping off
one's back.   The fingers itch to chip flints.   Time seems
to wheel backwards through the intervening cycles, and
we are again the contemporaries of primitive man.   In
this savage theology, this zoolatry, that sees divinity itself
—or emanations from divinities, or symbols of divinity—
in the beast-world, the fishes afford a very interesting study.
Throughout the Pacific, modern folk-lore is still the same
clan-animal worship that I have referred to in Chapter III.
The fish are lords of the sea.   In the Tongan, Fiji,
and other groups of islands, reverence for the whale and
shark, eel and sun-fish, and many another creature of the
waters, influences the daily life of the people, controls their
habits, and colours their thought.   Among tutelary spirits
—the "aitu" of the Samoans, the "atua" of New Zealand—
we find all the larger and more dangerous fishes ; and just
as in the Far West we find fish among the medicine-
animals and the totems of the Red Man, so in South Africa
we have "The Fishes" tribe of the Bechuana, the Batlapi ;
and among the tutelary "Kobongs" of the Australian
savage are numerous fish.   And with these, their habits,
predilections, and potencies, the modern folk-lore of these

people solely concerns itself. They think and live, in fact, in the old world of zoological myths.

To take the Polynesians only in illustration of the rest : fish and fishing are everything with them—their religion, their history, their art, their poetry, their daily life. They have fish gods, fish feasts, fish sacraments. In every-day matters, all quarrels arise out of fishing affairs, and every narrative of an incident commences "when out fishing." Similes of beauty and personal grace are drawn from fish. They use sea produce as currency, and divide off the water surface into individual holdings with the accuracy of land surveys. For are they not, after all, the descendants of fish themselves? and is not the earth, a gift of the sea, a fish also? One of their original gods was out fishing, and letting a hook—made out of a bone of "an ancestress" (fish-hooks are still made out of fish bones)—over the boat-side, hooked the earth, and drew it up to the surface. In the true spirit of zoolatry he returned at once to sacrifice a portion, but while he was away, his companions, unable to restrain their appetites, began eating the fish, which flopped and flung itself about. This accounts for the earth being so hilly and irregular. Had the hungry ones duly waited till the propitiatory "first-lings" had been offered, the earth would probably have been smooth and flat (as all savages would like it to be), for the fish would have understood that though it was being eaten, the proper formalities of respect had been observed, and would have placidly accepted the apologetic offering.

One of the most important incidents of their folk-lore is that which tells us how Kae stole a whale. Not that this cetacean lends itself very handily to the industry of the pickpocket, or seems a suitable article for stealing.

But then Kae was a magician. Moreover, the whale was
a tame one.   It belonged to the god Tinirau, who, when
visitors dropped in upon him, would occasionally hand
round bits of his pet whale, as our forefathers used to
hand round comfits, or, as everywhere in the East, the tray
still circulates among callers with the complimentary car-
damum or clove. And one day Kae whistled the whale
away from its master, and ate it up in the seclusion of
his own parlour. But Tinirau guessed where his pet had
gone, and told his wife, and she, with some of her lady
friends, went and kidnapped the magician, and brought
him back in bonds to Tinirau, who very properly put him
to death, and gave him "to the sharks and whales" to eat.

In another direction, the shapes of fishes, the Polynesians
have a lively mythological imagination. Why some fish
are flat is thus explained : Ina, the daughter of Vaitooringa
and Ngaetna, attempted to flee to the Sacred Isle.   She
had asked one fish after another to bear her thither, but
they were unable to sustain such a burden, and upset her
in shallow water.   She at last tried the sole, and was suc-
cessfully borne to the edge of the breakers.   Here again
she was unshipped, and the heavenly maid (tantæne
animis !) was so provoked that she stamped on the head
of the unfortunate fish, and with such energy that the
underneath eye was squeezed through to the upper side !
" Hence the sole is now obliged to swim flat, with one side
of its face having no eye."   But the day's work was by no
means over, for Ina now summoned the shark, and suc-
ceeded in reaching the Sacred Island. Feeling thirsty
during the voyage, Ina cracked a cocoa-nut on the shark's
forehead, and this accounts for the bump now found on
the forehead of all sharks, and called Ina's bump.

Now, though all this is as old as the hills, and older

perhaps than some, it is nevertheless modern folk-lore, and, though of course in a modified form, to suit other circumstances and conditions, is the prototype of fishing folk-lore all the world over. Away up among the icebergs live people as truly ichthyophagous as any that Pliny knew of, and to whom a single species of fish is as all-important as the palm-tree to South Sea Islanders, or the banana to central Africa. They look upon the land as a pensioner of the sea, as indeed they well may, seeing that not only they themselves, but their cattle and dogs, live upon the produce of the water. Their coasts and rocks are the home and haunts of water-powers, whom they propitiate by deference ; and the shapes of fish are explained by superstitious traditions as incredible as the incidents of Polynesian theology. But let us come nearer home. Ask the Scandinavian why salmon are red and have such fine tails, and you will be told that the ruddy colour of the flesh is due to the fact that the gods, when heaven was on fire, threw the flames into the sea, and the salmon swallowed them (indeed this fish is accepted by some mythologists as symbolizing fire) ; and the delicacy of the tail of the fish is explained to the Norseman by Loki having turned himself into a salmon when the angered gods pursued him. He would have escaped if Thor had not caught him by the tail, "and this is the reason why salmon have had their tails so fine and thin ever since." Or go even to Yorkshire, and ask why the haddock has those dark marks on its shoulders. You will be told either the old story about St. Peter, or else that when the devil, in order to bother the fishermen, was building Filey Bridge, he dropped his hammer into the sea. A haddock tried to make off with it, but Satan was too quick for the fish, and gave it such a pinch that no haddock has ever forgotten

it. And why has the stickleback to build a nest? Because
during the Deluge it pulled the tow out of the bilge-hole
of the Ark, and if it had not been for the hedgehog who
plugged up the leak with its own body, Noah would have
had an exciting time of it, baling out his boat.

Those who read these pages do not probably believe in
mermaids, or in the sea-cattle which they have helped to
herd ever since the days of Proteus, and long before that.
Yet the belief in the mermaid is a contemporary fact,
and in the British Isles too. From the Shetland Isles to
Cornwall, and in the Sister-isle as well, the coast is still
the resort of kelpy, and nix, and water-sprite; while sea-
bulls—lineal descendants of those sea-calves with which
Neptune terrified the hostile charioteer—and sea-horses,
such as whirled the car of Poseidon over the waves he
ruled, still come out on dry land in the Isle of Man and
the Hebrides, to the great annoyance of those who own
land-cattle. And what are these sea-things but the prin-
cipalities, and powers, and possessions over which the
Morskoi Tsar, the Water-King of Russian folk-tale, lineal
descendant of Neptune, holds the sceptre? In Ralston's
delightful pages we see him, a somewhat shadowy form
but a patriarchal monarch, living in subaqueous halls of
light and splendour, whence he emerges at times to seize
a human victim. It is generally a boy whom he gets into
his power, and who eventually obtains the hand of one of
his daughters, and escapes with her to the upper world.
And so through the cycle of the sea-trow myth we come
to our own coasts and our own day, and in the land of
Thule find the old, old fancy still in all its unmarred charm.
Along the sandy margin of the voes of Uist the beautiful
maiden still comes up from her home beneath the waves to
enjoy the sunshine, and if the tourist should chance to see

a sealskin or other " ham " lying on the rock, he ought at once to seize it, for there will come to claim it bye-and-bye the pretty Nereid to whom it belongs, and who, without it, cannot return to her caves and her friends. He must be careful, of course, not to jump rashly to conclusions, and carry off a bather's clothes, or some fisherman's oilskin laid down for a moment by the owner, who has perhaps just gone round the corner. But if he finds the real thing, it will all happen just as I have said, and the maiden will beg very prettily for her skin, and if he refuses it she will accept her destiny, put her hand in his, and if he does not mind being seen walking along a turnpike road with a girl in the garb of Eve, he may lead her back into the town and straight to the altar of the little church that overlooks the billowy sea where his bride's friends live—but which she, so long as he hides her skin from her, will never be able to remember again. But sometimes it happens that husbands of mermaids, grown careless by the lapse of time, leave the " ham " (as the sea-nymph's fish-tail covering is called) lying about in an attic or an unlocked box, and then, alas ! all is grief for the motherless bairns. For one unlucky day the wife finds her old garment, and there comes upon her the sudden recollection of another world which she once lived in, and a longing—that she cannot understand, and still less resist—to put on the familiar thing overtakes her. She yields, and lo ! in a twinkling, she has forgotten all her earth-life, her husband's love, and her children, and hurries away straight to the sea, and is gone for ever.

So "gone back to the sea " is a pretty and decorous euphemism for " run away from home."

To refuse to marry a mermaid, when in your power, is what no man should do who has any regard for his family.

G

For not only will he die mad himself, but he will bequeath insanity to his heirs for ever. Remember Duke Magnus.

So much, then, for modern mermaids and their kith and kin. Their cattle include both water-horses and water-bulls. These are still seen on our coasts. The former is a harmless and sociable beast that grazes with common cattle, but if any attempt at capture is made, it at once rushes over the cliffs into the sea. The water-bull is more troublesome, does much mischief, and even kills its terrestrial equivalents in combat. Before it disappears under the water it always gives a defiant bellow. By this you may always know a water-bull.

The world therefore is still young ; and coming to religious superstitions, we find the vestiges of an ancient fish-cultus in vigorous existence among our own fishing population. Some of the charms, incantations, and propitiatory offerings are very significant, and when the interpreter arises—a Tylor, or Lyell, or Ralston—large inductions of principle will be drawn from them and the great code of superstitious observances which influence both the social and industrial lives of these people, be shown in its breadth and length to be the survival of the zoolatry that still flourishes elsewhere in pristine force. At present popular superstition is a mass of unexplained items, but all the same they bring us, so to speak, face to face with the megatherium. Thus, ten years ago a herring-fisher was brought to a police court for repeatedly ill-using his wife. He admitted the conduct, but explained it was done, not from ill-will towards his wife, but to attract the herrings !

Is it due to the grudge, dating back to Paradise, and the day when, as the negro preacher said, "dat woman robbed de orchard," that fishermen consider feminine influences so sinister ?

In the Isle of Skye, if a woman crosses the water during the fishing, the luck is doomed. At Flamborough, if a woman happens to enter a cottage when the men are preparing their lines, she is not allowed to depart until she has knelt down and repeated the Lord's Prayer. In Lapland, the fishermen avoid spreading their captured fish on that part of the shore frequented by the women, as the next expedition would be a failure. In very many parts of our coast it is most unlucky for a woman to walk over the nets or any of the fishing-tackle, although they take a very active part in collecting bait.

Burn the teeth of fish you catch, or your luck will be bad next day—pins found in church make good fish-hooks—a quarrel on the beach, if blood be drawn, will drive the herring from the coast for the rest of the season (Scotch)—stolen tackle is lucky (Swedish)—herrings eaten on New Year's Day bring luck all the twelvemonth through (N. German).

Flamborough, by the way, is conspicuous for the tenacity with which it has preserved superstitions. As late as three years ago the fishermen would not put to sea if any one mentioned a pig when they were baiting their lines. In Scotland the salmon is equally unmentionable, and is only obliquely alluded to by a circumlocution. It is called So-and-So's fish. As being somehow connected with the powers of evil, it often receives for a pseudonym the name of the tax-collector of the nearest village.

The days to be avoided or selected for fishing enterprises are religiously observed. But the fisherman's religion is not always that of the Church, as, for instance, on the coast of Lancashire, where the custom is to set sail on the Sunday. A clergyman of the town once prayed against this breach

of the Sabbath, as he called it, but to neutralise his prayers
the fishermen made a small image of rags, and piously burnt
the parson in effigy.

At Buckie, not long since, the fishermen dressed up a
cooper fantastically, his bright flannel shirt bestuck with
burs, and carried him in procession through the town in
a hand-barrow. This was done to "bring better luck" to
the fishing. It happened, too, in a village where there
are no fewer than nine churches and chapels of various
kinds, and thirteen schools. Now, whence arose these
ludicrous practices and credulities? And how came "the
parson" to be a personage of ill-omen to so many fishermen? His influences are hardly less adverse than those
of women, and the practices which I have noted as connected with the ill-omen of feminine interference apply
also to the clergy. The herring all left one part of the
Irish coast because they heard the new parson say he was
going to tithe the fishery; and in Lapland and on the
coasts thereof fish need never be looked for where a
church is in sight. The Finns make the sign of the
cross when they catch certain species of flat fish, and the
Irish will not eat the skate (sometimes called the maid),
because it is supposed to bear a very questionable resemblance to some of the grotesque mediæval delineations of
the Virgin Mary.

The avoidance of the neighbourhood of churches referred
to above finds some illustration in the fisherman's belief in
the great quickness of the hearing of fishes. In Sweden,
for instance, the church bells are not rung during the bream
season, lest the fish should take fright; and where the
pilchard is fished, the people are no less careful of their
sensitiveness to sound. From this half-mystic belief in
the sympathies of fishes has no doubt sprung the idea

that they foretell the death of their owner by fighting among themselves in their fish-ponds. Oliver Cromwell's death was " foretold " by fish, and also that of Henry II.

As barometers and weather prophets generally, fish are of as much interest to the fisherman as birds, beasts, and insects are to the man of woodcraft, the trapper or the forester, and some of these traditions of prognostication are founded upon the experiences of many generations. Thus Wellsford, in his ' Secrets of Nature,' refers to several which are of great antiquity, and of which the following are of interest, if only as a sample of the sea-folks' weather-lore :—

" Porpoises, or sea-hogs, when observed to sport and chase one another about ships, expect then some stormy weather. Dolphins, in fair and calm weather, pursuing one another as one of their waterish pastimes, foreshow wind, and from that part whence they fetch their frisks ; but if they play thus when the seas are rough and troubled, it is a sign of fair and calm weather to ensue. Cuttles, with their many legs, swimming on the top of the water, and striving to be above the waves, do presage a storm. Sea-urchins thrusting themselves into mud, or striving to cover their bodies with sand, foreshow a storm. Cockles, and most shell-fish, are observed, against a tempest, to have gravel sticking hard into their shells, as a providence of nature to stay or poise themselves, and to help weigh them down if raised from the bottom by surges. Fishes in general, both in salt and fresh waters, are observed to sport most, and bite more eagerly, against rain than at any other time."

When they feel an earthquake, the Malagassies say " the whales are turning over," or " the whales are bathing their children." The serpent or dragon turning over and causing

an earthquake is a widely-spread myth, and the whale of
ancient astronomy is really a sea-dragon.

In medicine, fishes filled an absurdly large space, nearly
every species being, at one time or another, held a cure for
some impossible ailment.   Shark's teeth, rubbed on the
gums, helped children speedily through dentition.   The
liver of the Murœna cured poisonous bites.   The eyes
of pike, powdered, were wonderful in their effects—so
said the Duchess of Portland of merry memory.   Petted
as the lamprey once was by Rome, its supposed affinity
to the fabulous remora of the ancients has earned it the
reputation of being a thing of ill-omen.   Yet its fat
removed small-pox scars.   Fever is cured (in Abyssinia)
with an electric eel, and in Wiltshire with a common eel.
Rheumatism yields, if you cannot procure the hand
of a drowned man, to a rubbing with red-herrings ;
cramp (in Ulster and N. Scotland) to an application of
fresh eel-skin ; toothache (in N. E. Scotland) can be got
rid of by carrying about the person a piece of a dog-
fish, the fish being returned alive to the water after the
excision ; a sprain is cured (in Ulster) with eel-skin ; deaf-
ness by powder of eel's liver ; jaundice by applying a split
tench to the soles of the feet (Yorkshire), but you must not
forget to bury the tench when it is done with ; hæmorrhage
can be stopped with the brain of the same fish ; cancer
needs only a crab tied on to the spot to disappear ; hooping-
cough can always be banished by putting a live fish into
the child's mouth.*   This tradition is found, not only over

---

* An old fisherman, formerly well known at the Foye, Keswick, once
caught a fish, which he put into the mouth of a child suffering from
hooping-cough.   He then replaced the fish in the water.   He affirmed
that the fish gave the complaint to the rest of its kind, as was evident
from the fact that they came to the top to cough !

a large area of Europe, but also in America. A correspondent of *Notes and Queries* gives an account of a similar practice in America. " One morning, during the fall of the year 1875," he writes, " I was wandering along the banks of the Schuykill river, when a young woman, carrying a child two years old, approached two anglers, and asked one of them for a fish he had caught. Receiving it, she seated herself on the bank, deliberately opening the child's mouth, and, thrusting in the head of the fish, held it there, despite the child's struggles, for the space of a minute or more. She then threw it into the river." A turtle is a regular medicine chest. " The stone from its eye" is a specific for ophthalmia ; its legs will, by simple application, cure varicose veins ; its shell, powdered up with some of its liver, affords an antidote to various poisons. But even in this aspect alone, the medicinal fish-lore is far too vast for more than this meagre recognition here.

Of the origin of fishes, folk-lore is full of information of its own kind. That birds were once fish I have already noticed, and now that the palæontologists are agreed that the Iguanodon, that mighty eft, walked like a bird on two legs "in his oolitic pride and his bloom," the French tradition may help forward the derivation of the birds from the fishes through the great sea-lizards.

Eels are to be accounted for in various ways. When the Brittany fishermen happen to catch the " lotte " they throw them back into the water, as they are supposed to turn into eels. In England they are supposed (as in Yorkshire) to be bred from dew in the months of May and June, or (as in Derbyshire) from the hairs of horses or kine which drop into cart-ruts, or into drinking-troughs and springs, and there quicken after rain. The origin of this belief is of course obvious to those who have seen the hair-worm in fresh water. Soles, so the French say, are bred from prawns.

But, as I have said, the time for reading the true significances of these local traditions has not yet come. Folklore is still waiting for its interpreters.

APPENDIX.

—◆◇◆—

A SEA-DREAM.

I HAD to go on business the other evening, after the regular hours, to the Fisheries Exhibition. The public, duly informed by placards that "the Exhibition will close to-day at seven o'clock," had already ebbed out of the buildings, and, trickling away by a thousand rills, had disappeared into its hidden springs in the suburbs. The buffets were desolate and the sections a waste. Here and there a care-taker, with a scarlet badge upon his forehead, flitted through the gathering gloom, tapping and tinkering at the woodwork like some human woodpecker. Here and there an "executive," like some black-beetle creature of the twilight, hurried across the silent sections, his arms laden with papers. Occasional lamps threw a spot here and there into sudden reliefs of light and shade, but between them stretched long dim spaces of twilight, an eerie sort of gloaming in which all the exhibits conspired together to look mysterious. The stands of the boats had disappeared from view, and yawl and smack and canoe seemed veritably afloat. A doorway opened somewhere, and the draught made the fishing nets hanging overhead wave and wobble, and in the deep-sea gloom that surrounded me I almost began to fear that perhaps some mistake had occurred ; that I was really and truly at the bottom of the sea; when lo ! turning round a rock, I found myself suddenly face to face with a gigantic specimen of the thresher shark. Turning to retreat, I found a bottle-nosed whale barring the doorway, while some fathom and a half above me a Japanese spider-crab, with all its legs outstretched, was hideously floating down through the dim space upon my hat.

I sped on, narrowly escaping collision with a great white whale that lay glimmering under the shadow of the rock-wall and passing directly under an enormous ribbon-fish—a slab-sided ghost of misery—that happened to be crossing overhead. But in a few steps more I was safe, and sitting down, regardless of spat, on an oyster-bed, I looked back into the ocean cave from which I had just escaped. (Poets, I observe, always do this, as it gives them an opportunity of describing

the same scene twice.) Sounds of water trickling here, plashings
there, bubbling up from springs, or sluicing down the salmon ways,
filled the air, and every now and again the ear could catch the sudden
splash of pike meeting pike, or flurry of reconnoitring lobsters un-
expectedly colliding. Far away in the distance were lights and what
seemed to be human figures moving to and fro—Naiads and Tritons,
no doubt, but strangely provided, for folk of that kind, with long-
handled brooms and poke bonnets ; yet as I sat there watching them
sweeping the sea floor and dusting the rocks, with the figures of the
ocean-monsters looming up between me and them, I became aware
that the great sea-things were talking together. The white whale had
the floor, and it spoke in a dull, plaster-of-Paris voice, while ever and
again the husky voices of narwhal and shark, sturgeon and sun-fish,
speaking as one who was stuffed with hay might speak, murmured a
subdued " House-of-Lords " applause.

I caught but little of what was said. So many trout were hatching
in the ponds close by that it was difficult to follow the speaker. But
the drift of the bulky one's utterances was unmistakable. It was
grumbling consumedly. Whoever had heard of such nonsense as
studying the manners and customs of whales and sharks on dry land ?
Why was not the Exhibition held off the Dogger Banks in thirty
fathoms of good sea-water ? *There* was the place to see things as they
really were. The right way to study the manners and customs of a
shark (and the white whale was quite sure the honourable exhibit
from Otaheite would agree with him) was for the public to get into
water out of their depth, for he had been informed that sharks always
turned over on their backs before disposing of swimmers, and the
public would thus have the opportunity of seeing both sides of the
shark. At present they could only see one side, as the late Frank
Buckland had cemented the other down to the blocks they lay on.
Or how could any one arrive at an intelligent appreciation of his friend
the sting-ray unless they met him at home ? and what was the distinction between an electric eel and any other kind, if the former had
no opportunity of illustrating the difference ? " If the British public is
so interested in us and our ways, why don't they come down and see
us in our daily lives, let their children play with live lobsters in the
cracks of the rocks, tickle the torpedo fish, and play bo-peep with an
octopus ? They would learn more in one afternoon intelligently
devoted to romping with a spider-crab than in a whole life spent out
of water." At least so the white whale thought—and all the other sea-
things agreed with him.

Some of his remarks struck me as being both ingenious and just.

" The human beings," said he, "who have organised this exhibition
live on dry land, on the uppermost crust of it. Even superficially
measured, the extent of their habitation is far smaller than our own,
while in depth there is not any possible comparison. And yet they
have arranged this Exhibition solely according to their own divisions
of the surface of the dry land, instead of according to the divisions of
the sea. There appears to me in this arrangement an assumption of
superiority that is hardly warranted under the circumstances. Sup-
posing madrepores were to hold an exhibition, and to apportion off
the world according to the different varieties of corals ! Should we
not laugh at them ? Now, it happens that human beings cannot live
under water. Indeed, it has come under my own experience that, if
they remain beneath the surface even for a very inconsiderable time,
they die from choking." (Some whitebait began snickering at this,
and were suppressed.) "And the result is," continued the speaker,
"that because they cannot live under water themselves, they look at
everything from a dry-land point of view. Our marine industries,
such as sinking vessels or ramming them, the destruction of nets
which gives occupation to such vast numbers amongst us, the consumption of fish-hooks and angling-gear generally, and so forth, are
surveyed from a purely arbitrary terrestrial standpoint. Our marine
mysteries again—what can these land-folk know of them ? They are
actually discussing among themselves whether our life is, or is not,
' silent, monotonous, and joyless ! ' They are disputing, believe me,
as to whether there is such a thing as the sea-serpent or a cuttle-fish
big enough to seize and founder a yacht under full sail ! Now, if
these human beings are sincere in their desire for information, why
do they not let us organise a Grand Inter-elementary Fisheries
Exhibition, and, in a proper spirit of justice, consent to see things for
once from the sea-things' point of view? Think of the exhibits we
could produce relating to lives and ships lost at sea in what they call
an ' inexplicable ' way. Why, our Polar Expedition relics alone would
suffice to draw the whole world together to see. Who but ourselves
knows the true story of Arctic explorers that have disappeared ? Let
human beings, then, meet us fairly. Let them give over using the
word 'fishy' in the opprobrious sense they now use it. Let them
remember that the sea contains within it duplicates of nearly everything the earth contains, and a great deal besides that the earth
cannot match ; that though they speak of sea as an interruption to
continents, *we* look upon continents as interruptions to sea—good sea
run to land ; and, remembering all this, let them recognise the true

majesty of the water-worlds, and arrange for holding the next Exhibition—at the bottom of the Atlantic Ocean."

When he had finished speaking, the whole aquarium began firing
off motions and amendments, and as the electric eels in their excite-
ment began to get luminous, there was sufficient light to see the Irish-
member kind of scene that ensued. Each fish had apparently moved
that the Exhibition be immediately adjourned to its own particular
habitat, and as the fresh-water creatures could not agree with the salt-
water ones, they all began behaving like French Deputies. But the
sea-things proved, on the vote which was ultimately taken, to be
greatly in the majority, and though the fresh-water fish kept on rising
to questions of privilege and points of order, and otherwise obstruct-
ing, the original motion, thanks to the assiduous hammering of the
hammer-headed shark, was eventually carried.

It was to the effect that the next Great Interoceanic Fisheries
Exhibition be held in the middle of the South Atlantic—with an
ironical amendment by the white whale that if the site did not
commend itself to the fresh-water fish, they might hold an Exhibition
of their own in any "land-puddle" they liked. An executive com-
mittee was at once appointed, the Gulf Stream fixed upon as the
central office, the Sea-Serpent invited to be present on the opening
day, and the prizes scheduled. Gold and silver medals were awarded
for the whales that sank the biggest schooner and drowned the most
Dundee whalers respectively ; the same for the sharks that swallowed
the biggest man (if dressed in tarpaulins at the time an extra honourable mention) ; and the same for the sword-fishes that rammed their
snouts deepest into ships. The list was a very long one—for every
fish had a suggestion to make for its own benefit—and it closed with a
copper badge for the oyster that could choke an American.

All seemed happily settled, and the meeting was relapsing into
quiescence, when I became aware of a deputation of monsters in the
aisle on my left. It was the sea-animals, who had been patiently
waiting to see what arrangements would be made for them, and the
silence was now broken by the voice of an aged walrus hoarsely
inquiring whether he was a fish. A "movement," as the French say,
was at once apparent in the assembly, but no one replied. "For," said
the walrus, "it appears to me that, as I am fished for, I am a fish,
and entitled, therefore, to be treated as such." A chorus of approval
broke from the narwhals, seals, sea-lions, manatees, and dugongs, and
the argument finding no contradiction, it was agreed that some icebergs and other conveniences should be provided for the animals.

Upon this another difficulty arose, for the polar bear, who had walked over from the Terra Nuova annexe, gruffly put forward a claim on his own behalf. " This Exhibition," said he, " is not only for fishes but for fishers as well ; and though I should never think of asking any one to call me a fish, I am entitled to be called a fisherman." The outrageous bad taste of this aroused the indignation of the whole assembly, and calls for Captain Gossett resounded through the dim aisles. But the bear persisted that he had a right to take his place in any Fisheries Exhibition that might be held, and that the rights of his constituents deserved as much respect as those of any other community represented in the House. But the fish would not hear of it, and after what is called "a disgraceful scene," the sea-lions were deputed to chuck-out the polar bear—which they did.

I followed the party out of the building, and when I had seen the polar bear—still grumbling immensely and threatening public demonstrations when he got back to Greenland—balanced in his old place on the top of his pyramid in the Terra Nuova annexe, and the sea-lions on guard all round him, I turned back. But whether I missed my road, or whether the fish had had the doors shut, I could not find my way back into the convention. So I went home.

PHIL ROBINSON.

LONDON :

PRINTED BY WILLIAM CLOWES AND SONS, LIMITED,

STAMFORD STREET AND CHARING CROSS.

* 9 7 8 3 7 4 4 7 8 9 9 4 3 *